MW00613256

ADVANCE PR

ACTIVATE YOUR LIGHT

"Aubry Hoffman has not only written a masterpiece, but embodies a heal-ing transmission that resonated in my soul. The Light pours off each page, shining possibility, opening my heart, and reminding me who I am."

—**Andrew Sam Newman**, Award-Winning Author of the
Conscious Bedtime Story Collection

"The second I started reading the opening pages of *Activate Your Light,* an energetic 'YES!' reverberated through my body. Aubry Hoffman affirms the truth Lightworkers need to hear: radical simplicity, honoring our path, restoring joyously, and inspiring others to match our vibration. In her story we find our own. Hoffman's brave voice shows us the emboldened, aligned, joyous life that awaits us as we claim the tools in her chapters to return to our essence and shine!"

—**Rabbi Jessica K. Marshall**, Founder of Sacred Lifecycle Rituals

"In this book, Aubry Hoffman guides you to step into your own power and share your Light with the world. If you are looking to grow your capacity to heal yourself and others, this book has so many simple ways to learn how. Her authentic voice is truly an inspiration to all."

—**Skye Dyer**, Singer/Songwriter

"Aubry Hoffman has channeled a beautiful guidemap for tapping into our highest good. Her voice comes through as warm and sincere, and the book includes practical visualizations and affirmations for integrating the wis-dom contained within. I trust it will serve as inspiration for fellow healers who need to be reminded of what fills us up so we can serve."

—**Caitlin Gordon**, M.S., L.Ac.

"For anyone feeling called to help raise the frequency of the planet, this book will not only help you to embody your 'inner queen' so you can be of service to the world, but will also open new portals to heal your body and discover your soul family."

—**Angel Quintana**, Creator of *Holistic Fashionista* Magazine

"Aubry Hoffman is a bright light and shares her Light and how to shine yours in this eloquently yet bravely vulnerable and repeatable synthesis of many great healing modalities. In addition, she discusses, from her real-world experiences, easy-to-follow principles for activating your inner Light. It's a beautiful gift for the world!"

—**Kari Halvorson**, MS, LPCC

"What I know for sure is that we are all Lightworkers. Aubry Hoffman's book will amplify your brightness and inspire you to live more in that *truth of you* so you can fully serve others. Her book provides a path that will rekindle that inherent spark in you, even if it's only a flicker, into a brilliant flame. Shine on!"

—**Christine Walsh**, Author, Speaker and Money Empowerment Coach

"Aubry Hoffman's lightness of spirit and radiant love shine through on each page of this roadmap to remembering, brilliantly weaved with her personal journey of healing. Healing is a spiral—a process of remembering and forgetting and expansion and contraction. Hoffman's book provides simple yet powerful exercises and affirmations to help us return home again and again. She's a woman of strength and integrity, a beacon of joy and truth—a beautiful person from whom to learn."

—**Juniper Jane Manchon**, Juniper Moon Healing Arts, Healer, Teacher

ACTIVATE YOUR
LIGHT

upgrade your energy
to step into
your calling as
a lightworker

AUBRY HOFFMAN

modern wisdom
PRESS

modern wisdom
P R E S S

Modern Wisdom Press
Boulder, Colorado, USA
www.modernwisdompress.com

Published 2019
Cover design by Karen Polaski, KP Design
Cover image by mashe/Shutterstock
Author's photo courtesy of Tiny Dragon Photography

DISCLAIMER

MEDICAL DISCLAIMER

The information in this book is a result of years of practical experience by the author. This information is not intended as a substitute for the advice provided by your physician or other healthcare professional. Do not use the information in this book for diagnosing or treating a health problem or disease, or prescribing medication or other treatment. Information and statements regarding dietary suggestions have not been evaluated by the Food and Drug Administration and are not intended to diagnose, treat, cure, or prevent any disease.

For my son, Aspen. Being your mother is an honor.
You are a bright Light; may you never stop shining.

For Abigail. They tried to dim your Light, but they didn't know
they were dealing with a star brighter than the sun.
Thank you for being the catalyst that inspired me to write this book.

With much love + light,
thank you Abigail. ♡

Auby

CONTENTS

INTRODUCTION

This wasn't the book that I planned to write. I had planned on writing about intuition and learning to trust yourself because this is what I primarily teach online and on my podcast. This book concept came to be during a particular dark time in early 2019. I was being asked to face and heal from another layer of trauma from my past. I felt burned out and stuck and had no idea why I was doing what I was doing. I felt like I had hit a wall and had no desire to keep teaching and sharing the way that I was.

This book that you are reading was conceived on a much-needed spring break trip to the ocean. I would wake up early most mornings and walk along the beach. Each morning more of the book came to me. It felt like inspiration directly from Source Energy. At the time, I didn't think it was a book anyone else would read, because the guidelines and the messages I was receiving on my morning walks were *exactly* what I needed to hear. The Universe was telling me the way it wanted me to live and the guiding principles that I had to adopt daily if I was going to live out my purpose. The guidelines I was being shown were powerful healing modalities that I had practiced on and off over the past 15 years. I was being asked to turn them into a coherent method to use in my daily life.

I started to write the book immediately. I didn't have my computer on the trip, and so I started jotting down my outline on my phone. The words needed to come out, and they were words that I needed for my own healing. Over the next few weeks, I started putting into practice daily what I was writing about and something incredible started to happen. The cloud that had been hanging over my head for years began to lift.

I started making massive internal shifts with my energetic state and my thought life. I started attracting more and more clients for my healing sessions, and people started to tell me on a daily basis that I was glowing. And I was. As I wrote about what it meant to activate your Light, I was activating my own Light in a whole new way. I was preparing myself to step into my power and be ready to share the messages in this book with as many people as possible when the time was right.

I wrote this book for me, because I had once again reached the end of my rope and was desperate for some answers that would bring me energy and move me forward. In the process of writing the book for *me*, I was also thinking about *you*. I know I'm not alone in my gifts. I'm not the only powerful soul with intuitive healing abilities and a bright Light inside that longs to shine. I'm not the only one desiring to be part of the growth and expansion of love and healing. I'm not the only one who is an empath and tired and overwhelmed by the state of the world and how fast we move and how much stimuli are in everything, all the time. I'm not the only who has felt the call to shine their Light so that others could be healed and inspired. We are all connected, and if I needed this book, I know you needed this book as well. So I wrote it for me, and I wrote it for you, and I wrote it for all living beings everywhere, so that my Light and your Light can shine their brightest and in turn inspire and heal millions of souls in need of the Light of their true essence.

I wrote this book for Lightworkers everywhere because our time has come, our calling is clear, and the world needs our Light. I wrote this book as a gentle reminder to come home to your true essence, to connect to the Light of who you truly are and to shine. My method is simple and it works. As I wrote this book, I called on the great masters and teachers and healers throughout all time to come and be with me and write through me and for you. There is a palpable energy to this book that will inspire change, healing, and action in you and I am so excited for you to read it. No longer will you be held back. Your Light can no longer be dimmed. The world is waiting for your Light to burst out and shine and I know that you are ready. Shine, Lightworker, shine.

With love,

Aubry

PART I

LIGHTWORKER
RISE

FINDING YOUR WAY BACK HOME

"Your heart sees by its own Light.
In meditation, adore the subtle fire.
The Light that you see by
is the Light that comes from inside."

—**The Radiance Sutras**

I was sobbing. I had just put down the phone with my mother after she had shared new information about past trauma in our family. This news hit like a ton of bricks. *Why do I have to deal with this now? Hadn't I already healed?* I was being presented with another round of healing work to do. On top of that, I was tired. My days as a single mom seemed long, lonely, and exhausting. *Would I always be alone in processing so much pain and trauma from my past?* As the tears fell down my face, that old familiar feeling arose—the feeling of wanting to run away from it all and at the same time knowing I was called to be a Light. I was ready to share my healing work, and at the same time I was exhausted and didn't know where to turn.

You may feel similarly. You know you are called to shine, and still, the doubt and the feelings of overwhelm creep in. What do you do when you are stuck and tired? How do you step into your calling without feeling overwhelmed? After getting off the phone with my mother that day, I didn't know how to move forward. This was the low from which this book was born. The information I share here helped me to activate an energizing and healing Light within myself and it can do the same thing for you. It starts with remembering our true essence.

What is our true essence? I had to remember that at the core of my being there is nothing but pure Light. This "Light" is referred to in many different ways. It is called "A Higher Power," "The Divine," "Mother Earth," "God," "Source Energy," "The Universe," or simply "Love." I like to refer to it as Light because that is how it feels to me: a bright, guiding presence that clears away darkness. We connect with this Light when we let go of the stories we have about who we think we need to be to feel safe and loved. We connect when we choose to identify with more than just our bodies and minds. We embody this Light when we quiet the chatter and step into the present moment. This Light feels like home. Connecting to this part of us suspends worry and doubt, and we feel safe. Once you have had an experience with this Light, you can't help but want to share it and help others to come home to the peace and healing that is our true essence. This desire to share the Light is what makes us Lightworkers. Activating your own Light is ultimately the embodied experience of coming home to your true essence.

What Does it Mean to Be an Activated Lightworker?

Activated Lightworkers have a strong desire to serve by spreading the Light. Although they go about it in different ways, they don't serve by sacrificing all their own needs to help others. They don't serve to the point of burnout and exhaustion. They don't serve by giving and meeting the needs of everyone who asks.

They serve by being in alignment with their Light and living at such a high vibration that they teach, lead, and inspire the people in their sphere to match their higher vibration. This is a true act of service, to energetically vibrate at higher frequencies and stay connected to Source and invite everyone around to follow. Activated Lightworkers never tire from service because they have clear boundaries set up in all areas of their lives and they serve by creating space to be connected to Source Energy.

A person who has activated their Light is easy to spot. Not always because they stand out, but because of the way you feel when you are around them. A person who has activated their Light feels good to be around. To be in their presence is to feel inspired and energized. You feel Lighter simply by being in their energy field. You are unable to complain or stay locked into negative thinking patterns because a person who is living in the Light will immediately direct the conversation to what is working instead of what is not. They will direct the conversation to the solution. The conversation will prompt you to think about what you are grateful for, because gratitude is the state the Lightworker lives in when their Light is activated.

An activated Lightworker values being aware of what is going on in the world but refuses to contribute to the expansion of darkness by participating in conversations about how much resistance they have to what is happening. When the Light is strong within someone, they are interested in creating more peace, more joy, and more love with every word they speak and so they will listen with presence and speak with hope and actively talk about the solution.

When you meet someone who has activated their Light, you will notice that they have people around them who are also bright Lights. They will be surrounded by some of the most inspirational people you have ever met. An activated Lightworker is very careful about who they spend their time with. They have no time and space in their life for relationships that do not support their healing, growth, and evolution. You will notice that their friendships are supportive and the people they are in close contact with shine with the same bright Light and power that they do. They are involved in the type of interactions that spark creativity and create massive positive impact in the world.

Activated Lightworkers are highly intuitive. They live their lives connected to their intuition because they have made the connection with Source Energy their top priority. They take joy in the present moment, in meditating and any other activities that help them slow down and connect to the Light. They value personal growth and show up for their healing work because they know this makes their Light stronger. They love the process, they love the healing, and they love the climb toward expanded states of consciousness and freedom. They see purpose in the way they live their lives and they are driven to be of service. They serve by shining their Light and they know that they have to take care of themselves to shine.

Activated Lightworkers trust themselves. They don't spend their time looking for answers outside of themselves. They trust themselves because they are connected to their true essence, they are connected to their heart, they are connected to the Source of all Light, and they have learned to trust this Source.

A person who has activated their Light has a life that seems to flow with great ease because they have decided to step into the flow of life instead of fight against it. They expect things to work out for them and so they do. They are always looking for what is going right. They don't spend their time or energy focusing on what isn't working. They welcome failure and aren't sidetracked by the many ways that humans fail. They see failure as a lesson and pick themselves up and get right back in the flow.

Miraculous circumstances seem to flow to activated Lightworkers because they have opened the abundance tap in their lives. They have become grateful for the even seemingly small ways that abundance shows up in their lives. Their abundance just keeps increasing and they are able to share with everyone around them. They are abundance activators, and if you spend enough time with them, you will begin to see more to be thankful for as well.

A person who has activated their Light chooses love over fear every day, and it shows in the openhearted way that they carry themselves through the world. They are safe and protected because love is the most powerful force in the universe, and as they walk through the world *in love* they find love in every person, circumstance, and place. Love is their guiding force. Their actions, their boundaries, their creative projects, their choices, and their relationships are all infused with love and an open heart. Love is the energy that fuels an activated Lightworker and they know that love is available to them anytime they connect with Source Energy. Activated Lightworkers are lovers, and their love shines through in all that they do.

This life I'm writing about is *your* life, a life that you can claim over and over again as you embody the guidelines in this book. You are a Lightworker, and you likely picked up this book because you are ready to let go of ways of being that no longer serve you so that you can shine even brighter. You picked up this book because you long to connect with the real you, the you who is connected to everyone and is a part of Source Energy.

You are the Light. You came here on a human journey where we remember and forget (and remember and forget) our true essence.

Your purpose is to accept your calling and find your way back to your Light every single day; to accept the challenges and inevitable darkness that we find here on Earth and choose to do the work to embody the Light each and every day. When you embody your Light, you come home: home to your true self, home to your purpose, home to the essence that is really you. When you embody the Light, you shine so brightly that the darkness begins to diminish, and the expansion and evolution of all beings everywhere is served. Shine on, Lightworker! This is the calling to activate your Light!

CHAPTER 2

THE WORLD NEEDS YOUR LIGHT

"Our deepest fear is not that we are inadequate. Our deepest fear is that we are powerful beyond measure. It is our Light, not our Darkness, that most frightens us."

—Marianne Williamson

I describe my calling as a knowing; a quiet intuition that I am supposed to be doing exactly what I currently am doing. I have spent years running from that calling—working in jobs I knew weren't aligned, staying in relationships that dimmed my Light, hiding out in places too small for my spirit. All because I doubted my own knowing. *What if I mess up? What if I'm not good enough? What if I'm not OK?* Doubt still creeps in about my calling as a Lightworker, but it doesn't rule me.

I still remember the day a few years back when I was journaling after life had brought me to my knees again. I paused to look up at the sky, and in that moment, I knew I was done running. I knew it was time for me to step into my role as a Lightworker and push past the fear and doubt to shine. I started my podcast, *The Queen of*

Intuition, shortly after that moment, and I have never looked back. I had run away from myself and come back enough times to finally know that I was a Lightworker, and I was ready to shine.

Lightworker: Accept Your Calling

There is this thing waiting to burst out from within and shine its Light, but you're scared of what it means. What will people think? How will I support myself? You have no idea what the next step to take is, so you hide yourself in your busy schedule, your addictive patterns, the wrong relationship, or your limiting beliefs. You can hide for years, but your soul's calling to activate and shine its Light won't go away.

If you keep running from your calling, life will bring all kinds of things into your realm to wake you up and get your attention. This can manifest as loss of a relationship or job, pain in the body, or anxiety and depression. Finally, you will no longer be able to turn away from the constant ache of your soul to live its essence. You will have no choice but to step up and bravely accept your calling as a Lightworker.

The world needs your Light now, and you second-guessing yourself doesn't serve anyone. From a young age, many of us were taught to be good, stay quiet, do what we're told, and to not rock the boat. When you accept your calling as a Lightworker, this initial doubt will be present because you are breaking the mold, healing generational patterns of pain from your family, and declaring yourself to be a powerful healing being. You are here to usher in a new way of being for yourself and for all who surround you. Change, even positive change, brings with it resistance.

To claim your role as a Lightworker is to be a warrior. Regardless of the voices in your head that chant lies at you, regardless of what other people may think or say about you, you decide to rise. You rise because you know you are here to help usher in healing and restore wholeness to this planet. Regardless of your fear or confusion, you make a choice to ignite your own inner Light. The longing inside you makes it impossible to do anything but accept your calling. With bravery and passion you rise, standing tall and proud with an open heart and an open mind, ready to shine in a world that needs the healing presence of your Light.

Accepting your calling as a Lightworker means that you choose to live your life connected to your Light. It doesn't matter what you do for a living. If you're a scientist, teacher, therapist, or make-up artist, when you live connected to the Light, your very presence is healing to anyone that you encounter. Once you accept your calling, you will find that help shows up. The fact that you are reading this book means that help is already on its way. You will begin to feel more peace, ease, and flow in your life. You may not have all the answers, but you will feel like you are on the right path. Your energy will begin to shift and move into a place of greater alignment. The people and situations that you need to activate your Light will begin to appear. You will start looking for the signs. There will be a shift in your confidence as you claim your calling and start to activate your Light and shine for all to see.

Lightworker: Heal

The moment that you accept your calling as a Lightworker, you set in motion a powerful healing process within yourself. Healing isn't always linear. It isn't always logical or easy. As we step into our calling, our deepest wounds can rise to the surface for the first time or again after we thought they were healed. Your task is to embrace the darkness and ask for help.

Healing will come in waves for the rest of your life, but it's important to realize that the path of a Lightworker is first a path of personal healing that then will ripple out to the world around you. You will begin to see your healing work as part of your calling as a Lightworker. It's easy as you step into your calling to place all of your focus on sharing your gifts with the world. Yet your priority needs to be in tending to your own heart, acknowledging your wounds, and directing the powerful healing Light of your own being to yourself first. You are called to address your shadow and own with brave vulnerability your deepest fears and wounds. You see how your brokenness has made space for your full brilliant Light to come pouring in.

We address our own healing first so that we don't let our ego get out of check, so that we approach our calling as Lightworkers with humbleness. Our gifts are not something that we made happen; we are products of life and grace flowing through each of us. We must be careful not to lead as a Lightworker with a story of someone who has healed and has no more healing to do. We step into leadership as a Lightworker by being honest that we are on our own healing journey. You make your own healing work a priority so that your Light shines and you can give to others.

There are two tasks on the healing journey. Number one is to do to the work: to seek out the healers, books, teachers, and relationships that will help you heal and grow. The other task is a bit of a paradox, because you are asked to hold a vision of yourself as already whole, as already healed. Yes, there is work to be done, and your healing journey will continue to come in waves for the rest of your life. And there is also the reality that you are perfect as you are, that you are already healed and whole and a channel for Source Energy to move through and shine its Light. Lightworker, you are both healed and healing.

Lightworker: Unite with Your Soul Family

Once you have made the choice to accept your calling and heal, it's time for connection and collaboration. This book is a collaboration with you, so that together we can touch millions of people with our healing Light and inspire them to come home to their true essence. In order for you to accept your calling, to heal and to rise you must unite with your soul family.

Your soul family is waiting for you. This book will help you connect with them because this book will help you connect to yourself and align with Source Energy. As you align, you draw to yourself more like-minded souls. Your soul family exists to help you grow. Where other relationships may have distracted you or dimmed your Light, your soul family shows up to support you. You will know when you meet a member of your soul family because you will feel a deep, soulful connection immediately. You will feel supported, and your time together will focus on solutions and love and will help you connect to the Light.

Our world is fast and isolated, and now, more than ever, we need to connect with our fellow Lightworkers. The time of proving our individual worth by doing things by ourselves is over. There is no competition, and there is no room for jealously or feelings of inadequacy. These are old ways of being that must be eliminated for the work that lies ahead of us. As we connect to each other, we speed up the expansion of the Light. It's time to let go of any idea of separation and begin working together. When we work together our power is multiplied. In community, our healing speeds up.

It will be the members of your soul family that you meet along the way that will help you activate your Light. The journey you are about to go on will not be a lonely hero's journey, it will be a story of friendship and coming together. Our Light will only shine its brightest when it shines with others. Lightworkers, unite.

Your time is now. The calling is clear. You are here to help lead people home to their Light. You are here to help people step into their power and find freedom to live the lives they were meant to live. You have accepted the calling and set into motion a powerful healing process that can't be stopped. You are healed. You are whole. Your soul family is showing up and, even if you have only a few of them in your sphere right now, you will begin to see they are coming to you in a myriad of different ways. You were born at this time in history with a specific calling as a Lightworker to help restore the balance between Light and Dark, to call forth the Light in yourself and in others so that life can expand and grow, as it naturally desires. Now is the time to activate your Light and step into your full power.

How to Use the Practices in this Book

At the end of every chapter you will find a personal practice. These will include guided meditations, personal ceremony ideas, and other healing practices to help you apply the concepts in the *Activate Your Light Method*.

Each chapter will close with an activation code. These can be read anytime that you feel disconnected from your true essence and they will activate the steps outlined in this book in your body, mind, and spirit. I wanted you to have something you could come back to whenever you needed a reminder of what you learned in the chapter but didn't have time to reread everything. These codes are channeled reminders from Source Energy and are to be used for the good and healing of all and the evolution of our planet. You can go back and read these codes at any time for an immediate activation of your Light. Before you read them, take a few deep breaths and enjoy a moment of silence to ground your energy and enter into a receiving mode. The energetic vibration of the words in these codes is a powerful blessing to all who read them.

I'll close each chapter with affirmations that help sum up the main point of the chapter. All of the affirmations are short, making them easy for you to remember and recite throughout the day. I like writing affirmations on my mirror at home, jotting them down and posting them on my refrigerator, or adding them as a reminder that will pop up on my phone. The most important thing to remember when using affirmations is to be in a place of feeling good before you recite them. If you use them when you are feeling off, they will lack creative and healing power. To put yourself in a place of feeling good, move your body, rest, spend time with people you love, practice gratitude, or take some deep breaths and then use the affirmations. My intention is that these affirmations will cocreate powerful change in your daily life.

TRY THIS

Connect with Your Light Visualization

1. Find a comfortable seat and begin to breathe in a conscious and rhythmic way. Slow down your inhaling and exhaling and bring your attention to your heart. Imagine a ball of golden Light surrounding your heart. As you continue to bring your attention to this golden ball of Light, it grows to fill every inch of your body.

2. Notice how your body and mind respond as you focus on the golden Light emanating from your heart center. You may find that connecting to this Light feels familiar, like coming home. This is because the golden Light has always been with you and is your guiding internal Light.

3. You can return to this golden Light and feel it fill your being whenever you need to remember your true essence.

Activation Code

Encoded in these words is the wisdom and power of all the spiritual teachers and healers throughout the ages. Inside of you are thousands of Light codes that are now being activated. This book is setting in motion a process that will fill you with Light. The Light will be healing and will cut away from your life anything that doesn't serve you. You are powerful beyond your own understanding and your own healing work will keep you humble, open, and ready to serve. Lightworker, your activation has begun. Trust this process and know that you will be led by thousands of guides both seen and unseen. You have been called and have accepted your calling. Your soul family is arriving. Peace and love surround you as your brightness expands. You are safe and protected always. Let your Light burst forth.

Affirmations

- I am a Lightworker.
- My true essence is Light, and I know my purpose is to shine and to be a healing presence in this world. I accept my calling and am willing to do whatever it takes to activate and shine my Light.

CHAPTER 3

THE QUEEN OF INTUITION IS BORN

"Some days I am goddess.
Some days I am wild child.
And some days
I am a fragile mess.
Most days I am a bit
Of all of these.
But every day
I am here trying."

—S.C. LOURIE

I used to think I was special because of the intensity of my early years and the drama and trauma that unfolded. I used to think my story was more intense than most people's, and that that somehow made me different and unable to connect to others. What I know now is that my story is your story, and your story is my story, because we are all connected and what happens to one of us affects all of us. We each have our story and each of us has trauma that is intense and unique to us. Our job is to own our story and to heal; to let our pain be the fuel that lights the fire from which we shine.

We are all special. I don't feel lonely anymore, because I'm no longer playing a victim role and I'm not making up stories about how bad I had it. I'm not using my pain as an excuse or a stamp of specialness. I'm thankful for my journey and the way it has forced me to come back to myself and shine my Light regardless of the people and circumstances that have tried to destroy it.

My Story: Trauma, Addiction, and People Pleasing

I grew up in a verbally, sexually, and physically abusive household. It was confusing because my abusive father was also a well-liked pastor of a large rural church. I grew up in a small town where everyone knew everyone else, and so my dad was very clear that we were to let no one know what went on behind the doors of our home. My mother was stuck in a cycle of abuse and codependency that my five siblings and I learned to emulate. In addition to the abuse, we were all kept at home and homeschooled, and so life was not only abusive but also very isolating. I was confused for the first 18 years of my life. On the outside, I suppose we looked like a normal enough family, but on the inside we were all hurting and terrified, including my parents. It was in that environment that I became disconnected from my own essence. My Light was extinguished, and I spent most days talking myself out of what I knew to be true.

Looking back on my early years, I feel gratitude for the way that my experience has connected me to so many others in life who have also suffered. My pain created empathy and understanding for the pain of the human condition. I thank the depth of the darkness of those years, because it inspired me to chase after the Light. I encourage you to look at the pain and suffering in your own life as a contrast that showed you what you didn't want and helped direct you toward your own Light.

Throughout my teen years and into my twenties, I battled an eating disorder that I developed to help me cope with the trauma in my home. When I reached the end of my college career, I shifted from this eating disorder to abusing alcohol. I moved to New York in my early twenties and began a healing journey that I now see as divinely orchestrated. My twenties were very difficult. I continued to attract abusive relationships that mirrored my home of origin. I was a victim of rape and found myself in physically and verbally abusive dating relationships. I was working hard to connect to myself and break these generational patterns of codependency and abuse. The beautiful part of this story is that I am a warrior and every year I was healing. It didn't always look pretty from the outside, but I was committed to healing and finding my truth and I found that there was support along the way.

Healer, Heal Thyself: Call in Healing

In the midst of my struggle with an eating disorder, about halfway through my college career, I started asking for help. I asked for help in my prayers, I asked for help from friends, and I asked for help from therapists, teachers, and healers. I asked for help and was led to books, people, and places that healed me bit by bit. A spark was lit in me in my early twenties that continues to this day. It is a desire to heal no matter what challenges I face.

Personal growth and development are two of my top values because I have seen the way it has set me free and how it in turn positively affects everyone in my life. I started my healing journey with therapy and groups. I still remember my first therapist teaching me the HALT acronym. It is an acronym of self-care: Never let yourself get to **H**ungry, **A**ngry, **L**onely, or **T**ired. During the years that I didn't have money for therapy, I read countless books on healing and would attend free healing events and seminars. I filled journals, meditated, and made vision boards. I tried whatever I could, with the intention of healing and freedom. I made my own growth and healing my top priority. I left higher-paying corporate jobs for less-stressful jobs. I walked dogs, made coffee, and took care of kids so that I would have the energy at the end of the day to come home and work on myself. I was a woman obsessed with healing because I knew, as you do about your own life, that I had a calling to serve and share, and I knew that my own healing had to be my priority.

A big part of my healing journey in my twenties was dealing with the back-and-forth from intense work on my own healing to struggling with addiction and unhealthy relationships. This really shifted for me when I decided to address my relationship with alcohol at 28. Because I had done a lot of work and made a lot of progress, I no longer battled an eating disorder, and my emotional health was improving daily. But I had been unwilling until that point to admit I needed to change my relationship with alcohol. I was high-functioning. I went to work every day, worked out, and was eating healthy, but each evening, I would come home and drink at least a bottle of wine every night. Each day was a struggle because I was hungover and I was making bad decisions while drinking.

At the time, I had a friend who was sober. His story of sobriety resonated with me, and so I decided to quit drinking for a while and examine my addictive patterns and tend to the remaining trauma beneath them. With this changed relationship with booze and the help of a new and supportive community, I was able to address some of my deepest wounds that I had been running away from while using alcohol to escape. It was at this point that my healing went on a fast track. I started exploring new modes of healing like shamanic breath work, Reiki, somatic therapy, dance, and healing foods. I became a yoga teacher and started sharing my love of yoga. Over the course of the next few years, I grew into my true self in a whole new way and began to attract incredible men and women into my life.

When I got pregnant with my son at age 30, the timing felt perfect. All the years of self-work and healing seemed to be paying off as I started thinking about bringing a new life into the world. My son is now six and the healing continues. It's not like all the work is ever over. There will always be new layers to peel back, and I still work with coaches and healers today. My goal is to clear whatever it is that is holding me back from being the truest version of myself. My healing and growing will never stop being my priority. Today I work on myself because it helps me live a better life. I also do it for my son, so that he grows up seeing what a woman who loves and values herself looks like, and so that he will be inspired to shine. My twenties were about me, and rightly so, but as I near the end of my thirties, my desire to serve others on a big scale grows. My desire to inspire others on their own healing journey drives me to get up in the morning and get on my yoga mat and connect to my essence. I'm inspired to shine, so that you will be inspired to shine, and I know in this way the world will be a better place.

Accepting My Calling as a Lightworker

I have only recently fully accepted my own calling as a Lightworker. Even though my intuition had been telling me for years that I was meant to step out into the world as a healer and leader, I kept running from my calling. I wanted to stay small, because that seemed to be the safest thing to do. I have struggled with codependency and people pleasing, and so a huge part of me was afraid of what other people would think. I was frozen in place because I was too afraid that someone might not like me.

Life has a funny way of making it impossible to run for too long from your calling before you become very uncomfortable with the repetitive stories that you keep living. That day finally came for me a few years back when I was going through a breakup with the father of my child. I was contemplating becoming a single mom and figuring out what I would do to support myself. I would step back and see myself going into my fear stories about what I could do. None of my options included the online brand and business I have now. And all of the options I could see dimmed my Light. I sat on the sofa in my sunroom one afternoon meditating while kids played around me. In a flash I was given the inspiration for my brand, "The Queen of Intuition." I pulled out a journal and started jotting down all the ways I wanted to serve and all the projects I wanted to complete. This idea for this book was one of the things I wrote down that day. I also felt via intuition that I needed to be brave and step into my calling now or life would become more and more challenging until I finally decided to listen. My calling, the reason I came here, is to inspire Lightworkers: to remind people that they can trust themselves, and that by connecting to their true essence, life will unfold with joy and purpose. There is no turning back for me. Some days I wish I just worked in a flower shop or had some corporate job with benefits and a salary. I wonder what it would be like if my early years had been easier and I hadn't needed to embark on a lifelong journey of healing, one that I feel compelled to share with the world. Some days I wish it were different, but when I get quiet and tune in, I know that this work I'm doing is my destiny. I know that my Light is needed for the growth and expansion of all humans. I know that everything happens for a reason, and that my heart is open, and that there is a Light in me that wants to shine bright and bold and beautiful for you and for me.

Stepping into the Queen Archetype

I know that I personally have been called to step into and embody the archetype of the Queen. According to most Jungian physiologists, there are seven female archetypes, and you can play with and embody different archetypes at different times in your life. They act as mirrors to see what themes are currently playing out in your life, and you can gain insight by studying the shadow aspect of each archetype. The essence of the Queen archetype is leadership and loyalty. I'm sure I will find myself embodying different archetypes as I age, but the Queen represents my work in the world as a Lightworker. I have had to battle my own internal dialogue about my worth of stepping into the role and have been challenged to set up stronger and clearer boundaries with everyone in my life. I have been attacked more since embodying this role and seen people rise up in my life with clear intention to hurt me and belittle my work. When you level up, there are some people that can't or don't understand your path and I've been blessed with the opportunity to set boundaries and move on and continue to rise. My calling has been challenging and also nothing short of miraculous. I have had the most amazing healers and friendships continue to show up in my life. I have found a sense of purpose and joy that I didn't know was possible until I decided to accept my calling. My Light has been activated and will continue to shine as I do the work and follow the method that I have created for myself and that I share here in this book. This method came to me at a very dark time on my own journey and the guidelines are what keep me aligned, coming back to myself, and shining bright. I look forward to sharing the guidelines of this method with you and helping you to shine your Light in a world that so desperately needs it.

TRY THIS

Owning Your Story Exercise

A great way to step into your power is to honor how far you have come and send loving energy to your past pain and trauma.

1. Take some time to write out your life journey so far. Write exactly what you feel needs to be told. Write about the parts you are ashamed of, write about the thing you have never told anyone but needs to be heard, and write about what you are most proud of.

2. Read your story out loud to yourself. Before you start, set an intention to listen to your own story with presence, with no judgment and with compassion.

3. After reading your story, stand in front of a mirror and repeat the following: "I accept and send love to all parts of my past. I feel proud of all I have overcome and accomplished. I am now releasing whatever parts of my story no longer serve me. I release the need to dwell on the past and welcome whatever guidance or healing is needed for me to shine my Light."

4. Notice how you feel. Remember, you are not your story. You are not the things you have done or the things that have happened to you. You are healed. You are the Light.

Activation Code

Encoded in these words is the wisdom and power of all the spiritual teachers and healers throughout the ages. You will be granted the grace and wisdom to find your calling and the courage to accept it. You will be inspired and guided by the strength of your own internal Light. Ask for help as you navigate your calling and step into your power so that you can live out your purpose and passion in the world. You now claim your birthright of joy, health, healing, and love and step into your calling with ease, grace, and flow. You will be guided always.

Affirmations

- I am always being guided by my own inner Light.
- I trust my unique story and know that by sharing it without shame I can help heal others.

CHAPTER 4

EMBRACING YOUR OWN UNIQUE PATH

"You have your way. I have my way.
As for the right way, the correct way,
and the only way, it does not exist."

—NIETZSCHE

"Don't try to comprehend with your mind.
Your minds are very limited. Use your intuition."

—MADELEINE L'ENGLE

This book offers a practical process for overcoming any blocks that have left you stuck, exhausted, or overwhelmed. It shows you how to connect back to the Light and live your calling as a Lightworker. I call it the *Activate Your Light Method.* This is a powerful set of steps that I have been using for years to connect to my own Light. In the process of writing this book, I took these tools and arranged them in a specific order with each guideline building upon the next. By practicing my own method while I was writing this book, I embarked on a second spiritual awakening that brought incredible healing and Light to me as well as to everyone in my life. This method is simple and easy to follow, and if you apply the practices on a regular basis it will change your life.

Why Do I Have to Do It Your Way?

You don't! Before I share with you the *Activate Your Light Method*, I have dedicated a whole chapter to telling you I want you to listen to yourself before you take to heart anything you read in this book. Do you have to follow my eight guidelines to activate your Light? No! In fact, please don't follow me or anyone else for that matter. I want you to follow your own knowing. I want you to follow what resonates with you.

While I do believe that you picked up this book for a reason, I don't believe that my book is the right way or the only way or even the perfect way for you. You picked up this book because it resonated with you, and you are following your intuition simply by reading it. Chances are you will find some truths that remind you of who you really are and that will help guide you home to your true essence. You may find things in this book that trigger you because you are being asked to be honest with yourself, and that isn't always easy. Unearthing some of your fears and insecurities is good, because that is part of the healing and activation process. You are being asked to let go of old ways of being and your ego will contract and feel small and afraid so that it can maintain its grip on you. If this happens, I encourage you to keep reading anyway, and find the nuggets of truth that are hidden for you in this book.

This book will also activate in you a process where you will begin to expand and level up in all areas of your life. When this takes place, you may find that you reach your perceived upper limit, and as a result, you may try to self-sabotage in order to stay small. If this happens, I encourage you to work the practices in this book and continue to expand and shine past your upper limit, to continue to step into your calling. It may feel hard at times but that isn't a reason to put down the book. Getting out of your comfort zone is where you grow. For a few of you this book may not feel right. Maybe you aren't at a stage in your life where these guidelines apply to you, maybe my energy and words don't resonate with you, or maybe there is another teacher for you to follow. If you feel expanded and open in your body when thinking about putting down the book, then please do. Pass the book on to someone you think would appreciate it.

Navigating the Self-Help World

Trust your intuition before taking the advice of someone else doesn't just apply to my book, but to everything in the self-help world. There are thousands of books in the world of personal growth, self-help, and spirituality and you will only distract yourself if you spend all your time looking for the next plan, process, or teacher to help you. It is easy to lose yourself in the self-help world if you aren't careful. There is a shadow side that exists in the world of personal growth and development, and before I address it, I'll start by saying I'm so thankful for the self-help world and the books and conferences that have changed my life for the better. I wouldn't be where I am today without the teachers and mentors I have found through this world. I'm thankful for the brave men and women who have shared their stories with the world and taught some of the universal truths that can set us all free.

The shadow exists in the fact that the people that author the books and lead the seminars are people just like you and me, and they can make mistakes. The shadow is when you begin to trust your teacher's words and opinions before you check in with yourself. You can disconnect from your own powerful Light and you will once again feel lost. You will look for a new process or system to help you find your way. It's like trying to lose weight and always getting on the latest fad diet only to find that you are gaining weight. The same can happen in the self-help world. There will always be a new teacher, new process, or new conference to spend time and money on but if the process does not lead you back to *you*, then you may have become lost in a world of self-help and shiny promises of happiness and fulfillment that keep you feeling stuck and exhausted because you have failed to listen to the ultimate teacher, the Light within you. Getting lost in the self-help world can dim your Light and keep you small. You can prevent this by checking in with your intuition whenever you find a new teacher or book or set of guidelines. You will know you are in the right place, with the right teacher and the right information, by how you feel in your body.

Here are some great questions to ponder when it comes to choosing what teachers to follow and content to consume.

- Do I feel open, at ease, and at peace?
- Does the work connect me to my true essence and help me feel empowered to solve my problems in the future on my own?
- Do I feel loved or judged by the work?
- Does it resonate?
- Does the message feel like it is coming from an authentic place? Does it feel like it is coming directly from Source?
- Do I feel pressured to buy more or join something that doesn't serve me?
- Am I being told I am wrong or am I being empowered to expand and grow?

If you are following someone who tears down other methods or claims their way is the only way, I suggest that you walk away. There is no universal right way or wrong way; there is only the way that is right for you, the way that speaks to your heart, the way that empowers you. My wish for you is that you will find your way with the teachers that will assist you in finding your truth, stepping into your calling, and shining your Light.

Intuition: Becoming the Queen of Your Own Life Journey

> *"Practice listening to your intuition, your inner voice; ask questions; be curious; see what you see; hear what you hear; and then act upon what you know to be true. These intuitive powers were given to your soul at birth."*

—CLARISSA PINKOLA ESTÉS

So, what exactly is your intuition? Webster's defines it as "a natural ability or power that makes it possible to know something without any proof or evidence; a feeling that guides a person to act a certain way without fully understanding why." I like to call it "the knowing." I've spent the last year interviewing doctors, therapists, healers, authors, and teachers for my podcast, *The Queen of Intuition Podcast*, and I have asked all of them to define intuition for me. The common response I get is that intuition is stronger when you're calm and it is information that is available to you that is beyond the range of your thinking, logical mind. It communicates in different ways depending on the person. Some feel it in their body when something is off; other people describe it as a still, small voice leading them. Almost everyone will refer to it simply as a knowing.

A more scientific way to look at intuition is to say that it is simply information that you have received over the years from all the experiences that you have had. Some of the information is stored deep in your mind and some of it in your body. When you try to make a decision and you choose to slow down or tune in, you are able to access this stored and often ignored information to make better choices.

A more spiritual approach is that intuition is Source Energy, or your highest Self, speaking to you and showing you the way. When we meditate or tune in, we are accessing our highest Self, and the universal flow of life energy is able to speak to us more directly. No matter how you define it, ultimately, your intuition is your truth and your knowing that is wanting to be heard above all the noise and chatter of the modern world. Your intuition isn't fear-based. It is rooted in love and will always guide you in the right direction.

We are born connected to our intuition and to our truth; it is all we know as babies and children. Somewhere along the way we were taught not to trust our intuition. It could have been a well-meaning parent or teacher who told us, in an attempt to keep us quiet or safe, that what we felt or what we knew didn't matter. Maybe it's not important for the adult, but for the kid it is, and when adults diminish a child's big feelings, the child starts to second-guess what they know and the disconnection from their truth has begun. Those of you who grew up in a household with verbal or physical abuse knew something was off in your household from the time you were a young child, but generally you kept quiet or talked yourself out of the reality of your surroundings to stay safe, be liked, or simply to survive. This caused a painful separation from Self and intuition. The good news is that we never lose ourselves. We just lose the connection. The connection is always available to us. We simply have to remember to connect.

Finding *Your* Way

When I first moved to Boulder, Colorado, I found myself in a mecca of gurus and strange New Age practices. I tried everything from Tantric goddess women's circles to gong baths to hours in traditional therapy. A lot of what I tried I didn't like. It didn't resonate, but I felt like I should like it and learn from it because all these amazing, healthy, spiritual people were doing it. Why didn't I like it? Was there something the matter with me? I share this to let you know you may have to figure out what you don't like first in order to be led to what does resonate with you and to what actually does feed your soul. You may need to know what it feels like to say "no" to something "good" and "spiritual" simply because you know it's not right for you. You will eventually find your people and your community and your teachers, so don't waste any time trying to talk yourself into liking something or learning from someone if your intuition is telling you it's off. You will know when you have found a teacher or group that resonates. It's important to realize we aren't meant to walk this path as Lightworkers alone. If you make your connection to your Light a priority you can trust that the people that are here to help you are showing up even as you read these words. When you are aligned with your highest self you are able to clearly see the next step.

Once you have developed a strong connection with your intuition, you will be able to know what works for you and what doesn't. You will be drawn to what serves you. Some of you may find your people in the yoga community; the myths of the yogic gods and goddesses may resonate with you and help you make sense of your life story. Or you may attend Tantric goddess circles and connect with the Divine Feminine that way. Maybe you will simply find a book or therapist or energy healer that resonates, and that will make all the difference in the world. You may get deeply into motivational events and jump and scream and cry with crowds of thousands of people seeking change. My point is that when you begin a spiritual path, or even if you are in the middle of it, you may explore everything under the sun, but ultimately, you have to follow your intuition to figure out what works for *you*.

Preview of the *Activate Your Light Method*

The guidelines that you will find in the following chapters are practices that I myself use to connect with my Light. They are things I have been doing for years and Source Energy has helped me to put them into words with the intention that they will serve you. These eight guidelines I call the *Activate Your Light Method*. I am excited for you to delve into each of them further in the following chapters.

- Surrender to Source
- Ask for Help
- Embrace the Darkness
- Simplify Your Life
- Mind Your Thoughts
- Honor Your Temple
- Dance to Heal
- Replenish in Nature

The power to activate your Light is readily available to everyone. Enlightenment is here now, and it isn't just something for people who you perceive as better or more spiritual than you. Being able to activate your Light is a choice you can make every day. It isn't something you have to wait years to see happen. It will get brighter over time, and the more you consistently follow these guidelines, the more connected to your essence and personal power you will be. You picked up this book because the time is now to activate your Light; the time is now for you to unleash the full power of your potential onto the world. The *Activate Your Light Method* works best for those who have the desire to shine and the willingness to try new things. May you be granted the wisdom to follow your intuition as you step into your role as Lightworker.

TRY THIS

Create Your Own Intuition Ceremony

A ceremony is a ritual that is used to observe something of meaning to you. I suggest creating your own beautiful ceremony for when you want to get clear about what your inner wisdom is saying. You can collect things of meaning to you and create a sacred space in which to sit when you want to tune in. Things you could add to your space include:

- Cozy cushions or blankets
- Candles
- Spiritual texts that hold meaning to you
- Statues of deities that resonate with you
- Crystals
- Plants
- Items from nature that speak to you (pinecones, feathers, leaves, flowers, etc.)
- Journal
- Tarot or Oracle cards

Once you have created your sacred space, you can open your time there with an intention or prayer that will connect you to your truth. Take a few moments to ground your energy by consciously breathing. Then listen and pay attention to what you feel drawn to do. You may continue to sit in meditation or draw a card or pick up your journal and write. Trust that whatever you feel led to do in your sacred space will connect you to your truth. Creating your own intuition ceremony will send a message to your highest Self that you are committed to yourself and aligning with your own inner wisdom.

Activation Code

Encoded in these words is the wisdom and power of all the spiritual teachers and healers throughout the ages. As you read this, a new set of sensibilities is rising up in you. Your intuition is taking center stage. Know that you will be given the wisdom to know who to trust and where to go. You are waking up and connecting to the wisdom of the ages and to the power of your own inner knowing. You will be led to the teachers and healers who are aligned with your highest good. You can trust yourself.

Affirmations

- I trust my intuition and connect to my inner wisdom.
- I am being guided to align with my highest good.

PART II

THE
ACTIVATE
YOUR
LIGHT
METHOD

CHAPTER 5

SURRENDER TO SOURCE

"Therefore the Master
acts without doing anything
and teaches without saying anything.
Things arise and she lets them come;
things disappear and she lets them go.
She has but doesn't possess,
acts but doesn't expect.
When her work is done, she forgets it.
That is why it lasts forever."

—TAO TE CHING

"Something amazing happens when we surrender
and just love. We melt into another world, a realm of
power already within us. The world changes when we
change. The world softens when we soften. The world
loves us when we choose to love the world."

—MARIANNE WILLIAMSON

Eight years ago, I found myself in one of the darkest places in my
life. I was drinking more than I ever had. I was dating new men

every few weeks. I was running away from my life. Terrified to be alone with myself, I was an addict looking for the next thing to distract me. The actions I regret most in my life occurred over a five-year period in my twenties when I gave myself fully to my addictive tendencies. I lied, cheated, and hid myself from everyone I met. On the outside I may have seemed like I had it all together. I was working seven days a week and getting myself out of massive amounts of debt. I had friends and good jobs, went to yoga, and travelled the world. But on the inside, I was exhausted, addicted, and trying hard to get better. I woke up one morning and couldn't remember the night before, couldn't remember how I got home, and all I knew is that I had reached rock bottom. Nothing I was doing to improve or feel better or be successful was working. So I tried something new. I fully accepted where I was in life and I surrendered. I let something bigger than me flow in. I stopped trying to get better on my own. The moment I surrendered to the Light inside me, my essence began to shine, and my healing took over in a whole new way.

I had been in this place before. I was a college sophomore. I had locked myself in a closest with a huge bag of junk food to consume all on my own before I binged and purged. I had been trying for years to pray enough, meditate enough, and work enough to make my desire to binge and purge go away. There was something about that day, locked in that closest, that made me realize I would never get better by trying to get better. I had to surrender and stop trying to be good enough. The moment I had that deep sense of being done trying to get better all on my own and finally deciding to allow life to heal me, the healing came through me, to me, for me. I didn't have to try; I simply surrendered and accepted the help.

I still get to this place at times, though not in ways as dramatic as when I was younger. I'm thankful for the pain and addiction in my past and the way it helped me learn the path of surrender early in life.

When we stop trying, we come back to the present moment. We have stopped trying to figure out how to be good in the present so that we can control the future. You can't derail when you stop trying. Your purpose actually has a chance to enter you and move through you. All you have to do is stop everything you have been doing to try to get there. You simply show up for the moment and the moment flows through you.

Surrender is an opening to the possibility that there may be a better way to find freedom. Surrender is a willingness to drop all the stories we have about ourselves and be willing to listen to our internal guidance, which is bigger and more powerful than any of our of old methods of fixing and control. Surrender is when we stop trying to get better all on our own and we step into the flow of life and allow life itself, Source Energy, our Light, to show us how to heal.

My story isn't unique; it is echoed in the life of anyone who has overcome pain and stepped into their power. Great men and women throughout history who tell their stories of healing, as well as millions of others whose stories will never be known, all get to the same place. Humbled and almost destroyed by life, we finally give up on our old ways of doing things. We let go and surrender to life.

Your story could be filled with more trauma or less than mine. In the end, it's all the same. We get tired of trying and anytime we feel tired, overwhelmed, or alone we have the opportunity to trust that there is wisdom in releasing control and stepping into the flow of life. We can always let in the Light and connect back to our true essence. The truth is that we have to surrender to something bigger within us in order to shine.

Maybe your story involves repeated frustration at work, or feeling stuck in your relationships, or being home feeling lonely and wondering what you're doing wrong. Life will use all kinds of scenarios to get you to the point where you are done trying. You have to experience it for yourself to understand the shift.

The experience is often a deep and profound sense of relief. Relief that comes from knowing you don't have to have the answers, and you don't have to be impressive or successful. You only have to decide to let Light fill you. You choose to start living just for today and trusting the process. When we are wounded and tired from not trusting, we can experience the profound and improved difference that comes from surrender.

What Are You Addicted To?

When it comes to this first step, it's important to identify what you are addicted to so that you can easily identify what it is you are trying to control. Even though addiction is typically used to define dependence on substance, in this book I will use it to describe any habit that is used to control life. It's easy to place the label of "addict" on those who are actively engaged in abusing substances, but not one of us escapes the pull of addictive behaviors.

Many of us are addicted to helping people or giving advice in order to control the behavior of others in order to feel safe. You can be addicted to dating the wrong type of person or addicted to being a victim. I find that individuals who grew up in homes where abuse or trauma was present are addicted as adults to trauma and being overwhelmed, and continue to create a life where drama and abuse are present.

You can be addicted to food, shopping, work, people-pleasing, your past story, thinking negative thoughts, or controlling others. What are you addicted to? In what ways are you using your behavior to try to fix things, or trying to stay safe, or trying to have a life that you want? When we can identify our addictive patterns and own them, it becomes easier to identify when we need to stop trying and to surrender into connection with the Light. Remember, your true essence doesn't have any judgment about your addictive patterns. Your truest Self sees your addictive patterning as a doorway, an opportunity for the Light to find its way in. Source sees addictive patterns as a necessary step for humans living on this planet to be able to get to a place of complete surrender. Your essence wants you to let go of all guilt and shame about your behavior and simply allow healing, Light, and love to become your predominant experience.

At the end of this chapter, I include Light activation codes that you can read when you catch yourself in addictive patterns. These will enable to you to let go and let life love you and flow through you.

The Path of Surrender

The healing path requires that each of you journey to the darkness in order to let go of the resistance that prevents you from embodying the Light. You must become familiar with fear, failure, and discomfort. You must fall into addictive patterns and coping mechanisms in order to see how incredibly useless it is to try to be good enough. If you are lucky enough to be truly miserable, you will be faced with one option: to surrender. You will allow life to carry you home to yourself.

I call this "the path of surrender," but really it is the beauty that inevitably can be found in the destruction. It is the gem hidden in the suffering. When we are stuck in trying mode, we build up what looks like a dark screen that covers up our true essence. In striving, we block our truth and we dim the Light. In an effort to be good enough, we numb our bodies, the very mechanisms that allow our inner Light to activate. Our plans and procedures and regimented attempts to prove that we are doing the work actually distract us from our own Light.

You will never figure it out as long as you're trying to be good enough for the next time around. You won't feel safe by trying to control life with plans, routines, or rules. Your power and healing lie in deciding to stop trying to live your best life and instead to surrender and allow your purpose to come and live through you. We can give up, over and over again if need be, until our experience with the Light captures our hearts and we don't fall as often back into our old ways of control.

The next time you are confused and hurting, my hope is that you will consider trying something new. You will stop resisting what is, and you will admit that your life has become unmanageable. Suffering can ultimately lead to a spiritual awakening; pain can lead us to the Light. The only way to fully activate and embody our Light is to accept what is and to surrender.

After we decide to stop trying, the real magic of living begins. When you become aware of your process, you will notice that the first place you sense a difference will be in your physical body. Your shoulders will relax and your belly will become soft. Your head may stop aching and you'll sleep better. You'll eat more or less, depending on what your body needs. You'll be more or less active depending on what extremes your body went into when you were in trying mode. A body that has stopped trying will often look younger, more relaxed. You will literally begin to glow, and you will notice a sparkle in your eyes and a new energy will come into your entire system.

It takes a lot of energy to try to manage your life, and for most of us stuck in trying mode, we are often busy trying to control other peoples' emotions and reactions in order to manage our own success and safety. When we let go of our need to try, we free up a lot of our energy and open up to the flow of more Light and energy coming in, and this is how we begin to glow. You will literally notice that people may do a double take when they see you or they may even tell you that you're glowing.

The glow comes from flowing with life and letting life flow through you. Imagine the last time you were floating in a pool or bath. Remember the way your own body released into the water, the way that relaxation took over. This is what is available to us when we stop trying. The more often we can embrace the suffering and confusion we are being given and see we are being forced by life to stop trying, the more we are able to connect to our inner Light. By connecting to our Light, we activate a Light inside of us that gets easier and easier to connect with over time. This is the new paradigm. This new way of being in the world will be what saves us. Our Light is the healing balm this planet needs.

Light Doesn't Hold Grudges

It is important to know that your highest Self, your Source Energy, your Light, doesn't hold grudges. Your Light isn't concerned by your behavior. In the realm of Light, there are no rewards for being good or punishments for being bad. There is only Light, love, and healing. You were raised to believe that trying hard and good behavior equals safety, love, and success. This isn't true. Our deepest feelings of love, safety, and purpose will come when we give up these old ideas of what we need to try to do or be in order to be okay. True peace and joy will come when we stop trying to be good and start allowing Light in.

If we think that our behavior is tied to our worth, it will be very hard to let go of guilt, shame, and worry about our past or possible future behaviors. Our Light doesn't care about our perceived mistakes; our true essence is the part of us that truly loves and appreciates all parts of us, including our shadow. To activate our Light and embody our true essence, our highest Self wants us to know we are worthy, regardless of what we do or don't do. We matter, regardless of what we figure out or what we achieve in the physical plane in this lifetime. Our Light wants us to know the ease and flow that is possible while living as a spiritual being on this physical planet earth. Don't waste time feeling bad about what you have done. You make peace if you can, you apologize where needed, and then you move on, realizing that as you let go and stop trying, the healing Light that will shine out from you as a result is all that really matters.

Your true essence, or Light, doesn't keep track of how many times you have failed and have had to come back home to yourself. The Light isn't impressed with your morning routine, your prayers, or really, any of your actions. Your essence is only interested in how much room you will allow for ease and abundance to flow through.

Surprisingly, your essence is at peace when you experience perceived failure or suffering because your highest Self knows that suffering is a quickening, an opening for the Light to come pouring through. What you experience as something to be guilty or ashamed about, your essence finds exciting because it knows you are being directed back home. Home is the seat of your soul, your Light, your truth, the reason you came here. It can only be accessed when you stop trying to figure out how to be good enough to be loved. Guilt and shame can be vehicles that take us right to the point of surrender. Surrender is an opening, a doorway for the Light to come in and for your true purpose to be lived out. Our purpose is ease, flow, and shining bright the Light of our souls.

The world needs our Light. She needs us to be in flow, to live with ease. Can you sense the invitation from your soul? Your essence, the Light, is speaking to you through your exhaustion and being overwhelmed, asking you to step into the flow so that our planet and everyone on it can heal.

Just for Today = The Formula for Surrender

"Just for today" is how we stay in the flow. It is the mantra we use to keep from falling back into old patterns and ways of being that no longer serve us. This phrase assists us in not getting overwhelmed by the days ahead or the severity of our wounding.

Just for today we choose to stop trying.

Just for today we choose to let go.

Just for today we choose to step into the flow of Light.

Just for today we give up control.

Just for today we trust life.

Just for today we let Source heal us.

Just for today we embody our true essence and let healing find us.

"Just for today" is a mantra I adopted years ago when I began to change my relationship with alcohol. It works. And not just in recovery. It works in every area of your life. Let this simple saying help you activate the first step, this necessary ingredient in coming home to yourself and embodying the Light.

TRY THIS

Surrender Practice

This is a simple, quick practice you can do daily to help you connect to your Light. Rub your hands together and notice the heat begin to build between your hands. Bring your hands together at heart center and say this simple mantra:

> *Just for today I will stop trying and surrender my need to control.*
>
> *Just for today I will connect to my Light and allow it to flow through me.*
>
> *Just for today I will admit where I am letting my addictive patterns take over.*
>
> *Just for today I will let go of guilt and shame.*

Activation Code

Encoded in these words is the wisdom and power of all the spiritual teachers and healers throughout the ages. The time is now for you to step into your power by giving up your need to control once and for all. You do not need to suffer any longer by trying to be good enough or get it right. You now see the incredible Light of your own essence, and it wants to fill you with its power and move you, live you, breathe you. Do you feel the Light as it enters you and flow through you, cleansing you, healing you, shining through you? When you try to control, you step out of the channel of Light that is flowing down from Source, from the channel of Light that is you.

This mantra will shift you into the flow of Light, into the stream of life. You are nothing but Light. You no longer have a desire to figure out how your life will go or try to be good enough to have safety or success. You are freed from the illusion that effort is needed to live your purpose. Your purpose is for you to step into the Light and let the flow of Light through your body be what lives out your purpose. You can't derail it; the Light is flowing through you, for you, for us all.

Affirmations

- I am free from the illusion that effort is needed to live my purpose.
- I surrender to the Light and let it flow through me and heal me.

CHAPTER 6

ASK FOR HELP

"We begin to see that we are spiritually linked with people halfway around the world, and with those who lived hundreds, even thousands of years ago. We begin to see that we emerge from, and are the expressions of, a single consciousness that is limited by neither time nor space."

—HAL ZINA BENNETT

When I found out I was pregnant, I was terrified and excited. I had just broken up with my child's father and moved away from my family and friends and felt totally alone. I knew that I was supposed to have the baby, even though I didn't understand why it was happening like this. I remember sitting on my yoga mat after meditating with tears streaming down my face. I didn't want to be a single mom. I didn't want to feel so alone, and I knew I wanted to do things differently than my parents. I started asking for help. It started as a simple prayer. I remember I had a statue of Quan Yin (the goddess of mercy and compassion) in my yoga space and I sent out a simple request to her and to whatever spirits, guides, or positive energies were available to help me. I was desperate for help and trusted it would show up. The clarity was immediate. I had the thought come into my mind of the very next thing I needed to do, which was to check out the local prenatal studio. There I found friends and teachers to walk me through my pregnancy in a very conscious, spiritual way. Help started popping up all around me, and I knew I was being divinely guided. A friend handed me the only pregnancy prep book I ever read, *The Continuum Concept*, and it gave me a beautiful groundwork for raising my son. I started to feel connected to nature and Spirit in a way I never had before, and my loneliness washed away. I felt deeply connected to my baby's highest Self and would often ask him what he needed me to do in order to best prepare him for his life here. My inner Light was activated without me even realizing it, because I had asked for help and trusted that it would show up.

When you are trying to control life all by yourself, you block the help and abundance that is waiting to come in so that you can expand. Once you have stopped trying, you realize how important it is to ask for and receive help with no guilt. If you don't ask for help, you will fall right back into trying mode and block the full brilliance of your Light. Our culture has taught us that independence is to be applauded, and that you are safer and more powerful if you go it alone. In order to activate your Light, interdependence is a necessary step. Connection breeds expansion. Connection is initiated by a simple cry for help, and this cry for help is accompanied by a deep sense of self-worth and a belief in the giving, abundant, expansive nature of our being. You ask, you connect, and you expand. This simple formula will always give you the space and freedom to shine as the brightest version of yourself.

Believing You Are Worthy of Help

You were likely programmed to believe that you deserve help only if you have done the right things and enough of them. In the *Activate Your Light Method*, I am asking you to begin to adopt the belief that you deserve help and a joyful life simply because you exist. It's hard to ask for help if you don't think you should need help, or if you only think you deserve help if you're being good enough to receive it. Everyone is worthy of help, and with your acceptance of help comes a level of responsibility to fully allow the help to come in, so that you can then pour it out again for all who cross your path. If you feel alone, you know that you are disconnected from your true Self. Separation is an illusion that keeps us locked up as dim versions of ourselves. In reality, you are surrounded with support in ways seen and unseen. Legions of beings and guides are waiting to assist you on your life journey, and all you need to do is ask.

Lack Mentality Affects Help

If you are stuck in a lack mentality about life, thinking that there are limited resources to go around, then you will want to hoard or hold onto any help that you receive. The flow includes allowing, receiving fully, and then giving. The cycle then repeats. But if you forget to only loosely hold the help you are given and pour it back out, you will inevitably block the flow of help. In order for you to activate a constant stream of support into your life, you have to question your ideas about how much help is available to you. To believe help is always available is to also believe in an abundant universe. A universe that believes in life, growth, expansion, and joy and is willing to cocreate that with whoever chooses to embody the belief of abundance and claim it for themselves. Someone with an abundance mindset believes:

- There is more than enough to go around.
- They are worthy of abundance regardless of what they have or haven't done.
- The more you allow in, the more abundance is created.

Source Energy, the source from which we all originated and to which we will all return, wants you to understand that its supply of energy and abundance is always growing and expanding. Source Energy wants to expand and desires its Light to spread and permeate every corner of existence. This can only happen when you allow in abundance, when you fully let it fill your being and then expand it back out. Source Energy can only expand if we allow abundance in. Source wants to expand Light, peace, and prosperity to all, and in order to do that, we need to allow more in. We need to welcome help in all its many forms. We need to ask for abundance to come pouring into every area of our life, and as we do that, Source Energy expands, Light expands, healing expands, love expands, and we become cocreators of life's desire to see how good it can get for everyone.

How Help Shows Up

One of the reasons that we block the flow of help and abundance in our lives is because we are only looking for a certain kind of help. It's usually the kind of help that we *think* we need. For example, if you are struggling financially, you may think that you need a cash infusion and become so fixated on help showing up in the form of physical cash that you miss the hundreds of other ways that help is showing up for you. Help can often show up as a difficult situation or what may be perceived as suffering. Loss is often a form of help. It can be the loss of a job, marriage, friendship, or opportunity. You don't have to look at failure and loss as negative. You can accept it as help that is opening the way for massive growth. Help can show up as people in your life that love and care about you as well as people you don't know who show up when you need them most.

Help also shows up in the spiritual realm as spirit guides, intuitions, visions, animal spirits, tree spirits, and oracles. If you are open and ready and willing to meet these guides, they will begin to show up. They are grandmothers, angels, goddesses, and gods; they may be healers and teachers, or enlightened beings that wish to assist all of us who live on the Earth plane now. To receive this type of guidance, you have to suspend disbelief and be open to things that may not make perfect sense. This is often a natural occurrence when you have reached exhaustion and are overwhelmed and have stopped trying. When you have exhausted your range of control, you are willing to open to things beyond your own understanding. You may have already had experiences with the Spirit world and know what I'm talking about. If you haven't, please know that everyone's experience is different, and the way that you connect and see your guides will be uniquely yours. This type of guidance is waiting to be called in. It can help you feel connected, remind you of your true essence, give you a preview of what is to come, and help you understand your past lives and experiences. This guidance and support can assist you in not feeling lonely, overwhelmed, or anxious, and it can communicate messages to you from Source Energy.

In order to connect to the Spirit realm, you must slow down and become quiet enough to meet those who are here to help you. It starts with a simple request that can be spoken or written down. You first ask with trust to be introduced to those in the Spirit realm that can help you as you activate your Light. Then you wait, knowing that help will arrive. These beings may show themselves to you in a dream, during meditation, or through a psychic or guide. They can speak to you through tarot cards or oracle cards. If you are ready and open to connecting to the immense amount of help from the unseen realms, begin by simply asking and being open to the way the message arrives.

A PRAYER FOR HELP

I call on the beings of Light and love that have come before me and that are here with me now. I ask that any incompatible energies leave me now, and that only forces that exist for my Highest Good be present. I call in protection, clarity, joy, and peace of mind. I can no longer do this alone, and I ask with belief and an open heart for help. I pray for the clarity and wisdom to see the help that is being presented and the willingness to receive. Thank you.

The help you are asking for can show up through your own intuitive wisdom. This is where learning to trust yourself and tuning in to your intuition is key. I have taught thousands of people all over the world to tune in to their intuition. I believe that the answers you are seeking begin with tuning in to your own truth. The process I teach is simple. It involves slowing down and listening to that still, small voice inside. It requires you to take a leap of faith and trust what you know to be true even if it doesn't make sense to anyone else. The more that you act on the guidance of your own inner knowing, the faster you will build a strong relationship of trust with yourself. This relationship of trust is the basis of your own intuitive knowing. Similar to the way your Spirit guides will speak to each of you in different ways, your own intuitive wisdom will show up differently for each of you. Your knowing may show up as a feeling in your body, an image that pops into your head, or simply an awareness. It will be your intuitive wisdom that will help guide you to the help you need or enable you to solve the problem for yourself.

TRY THIS

Create a Help Toolbox

Create your own mental wellness toolbox, a list full of people and practices that you can turn to when you need help. Write down practices that resonate with you on a piece of paper and keep it somewhere easily accessible. It helps to write down the items in your toolbox. You will begin to feel empowered with all the tools and people available that sometimes we forget about when we are in a state of exhaustion.

Your toolbox could include:

- Talking to people you love and trust
- Listening to audio meditations
- Watching videos online of spiritual teachers that inspire you
- Practicing breathwork
- Rereading parts of books that have helped you
- Scheduling an appointment with a therapist or healer

Your toolbox will continue to grow as you continue on your spiritual journey. Over time, you will begin to see that you are always supported and that there are countless ways to help yourself and people that love to help you.

Activation Code

Encoded in these words is the wisdom and power of all the spiritual teachers and healers throughout the ages. Source Energy says, "I am here to help you. There isn't anything going on with your life that does not have a solution. The solution is abundance and for the joy and expansion of all beings. I wish to bring you guides from the Spirit realm to protect you and inspire you. I will bring you help on the physical plane as well. You will be given exactly what you need, though not always what you want. Look for the people that will show up, look for the signs, and know that your needs will always be taken care of. I ask you to trust, relax, open, receive, and expand. This process will be one of ease and flow. There is so much I want to give you; I only ask you to keep your eyes and senses open so that you do not miss how much abundance and energy is pouring your way. Do not be afraid. There will always be help."

Affirmations

- I am worthy of help regardless of my past, my actions, and my family. I am worthy simply because I exist.
- I am open and willing to receive abundance, miracles, and help in whatever form they show up.

CHAPTER 7

EMBRACE THE DARKNESS

"The dark within my dark
Is where I found my Light
The fruit became the doorway
And now it's open wide"

—TREVOR HALL

I was years into one of the longest romantic relationships of my life and I was terrified. Long-term relationships always scared me because the long-term relationship I had seen growing up was abusive and unhealthy. I walked around in a state of underlying fear. My jaw would clench and my shoulders would tighten whenever my partner came home. The reality of my relationship was that I was safe, though I never felt safe and I didn't understand why. I didn't want to give it much thought. I had already done so much healing work. I wanted my relationship to work and so I was simply going to make it work. I tried being positive. I would write affirmations about how I wanted our relationship to be. We went to couples counseling. I tried filling our life with fun things to do and exciting travel adventures. I didn't want to admit I had to go back and work through more of the pain from my past. Luckily, I became so anxious that I was forced to look at the darkness from my past and the way it was impairing my ability to have healthy relationships. I started asking around and found a well-trained, somatic trauma therapist who could help me revisit my past in a safe way. She helped me with some of my most painful memories, memories I had been running from for years, and helped me to feel safe for the first time. I spent a year looking at the darkness from my past. I wasn't in a dark place the whole time, but I had to show up every week and face the unpleasant feelings I had been trying to cover up with positive affirmations.

To activate your Light, you must journey through your darkness. The darkness is anything that you don't want to look at because it is too painful, confusing, or uncomfortable. Instead of turning away from your darkness, you become curious about what it wants to show you about where you may need healing. You ask the shame what it needs; you humbly admit how powerless you feel over your addictive behaviors, and you own all the times you have caused others harm. To embrace your darkness is to embody humility. The moment you begin to own your darkness you will feel deeply connected to the rest of your human family.

Some spiritual communities have a term they use called "spiritual bypassing." This is when you ignore your own darkness and pretend to embody and teach the Light without facing your shadow, the parts of yourself that you prefer not to see. You know that you are around a person or an organization that is stuck in spiritual bypass mode when you feel judged. You can also self-identify yourself as spiritually bypassing if you are trying to ignore your own darkness and find yourself placing judgment on those around you.

There is no space for judgment when you have journeyed to the darkness of your own heart and understand your own capacity for harm. Many of us are under the illusion that we can control our darkness or make it go away if we pretend it isn't there. This tactic will only result in secrecy and a great deal of energy being exerted to try to maintain an appearance of the absence of darkness. The energy it takes to deny your own darkness can manifest as disease in your body, or an eventual imploding where the darkness takes over as continual self-harm or harm caused to others. If you are ready to embrace your own darkness so that you can live fully in your Light, you must realize your Light cannot exist without your darkness.

Dark and Light are the Same

You are not better or more highly evolved because you are a Lightworker. You would not be able to shine as brightly as you will in this lifetime if it wasn't for the darkness. Without the darkness, there is no Light to embody. With this understanding, we can walk through our lives without judgment or fear because we know that everything is serving us. Everything, even the things that seem cruel and unimaginable, is answering the cry for expansion. The greater the darkness, the brighter the Light. This is the paradox we must accept.

Dr. Wayne Dyer taught me through all of his incredible books that "what you resist persists." I believe this applies to darkness as well. When we resist the darkness by trying to fight it, ignore it, or make it go away, it only grows more powerful and the balance of Light and Dark is disturbed. When we embrace and accept the darkness, the balance is maintained and Source Energy continues to expand. Your job as a Lightworker is to aid in the expansion of Light. You must embrace the darkness instead of fighting it, or you will only be contributing to the imbalance that currently exists. The moment we all begin to embrace the darkness without labeling it as bad is the very moment that massive expansion, growth, and healing will happen for us all. By owning our shadows and walking without fear into the deepest, darkness parts of our beings, we are fulfilling our calling and Light expands.

Embrace the Darkness Without Getting Lost in Despair

The first step in embracing the darkness is to feel it, and the best way to fully feel and move it through our experience is to notice where you feel it in your body. How does the darkness feel in your body? Maybe you have never allowed yourself to feel it in your body. To really feel our darkness, it is best to find a safe place. You may even need the support of safe people as you journey into the waves of pain and fear that can course through your body. You stay with the darkness and follow what arises. It could be tears and screams or body movement. You may even have had a conversation with the darkest parts of yourself; with the shame, guilt, regret, loss, or whatever it is that comes up for you. Intense feelings come in waves, and when we give them the attention and respect that they are asking for, the intensity wanes and the strength of our Light increases. The key is to not get stuck in despair. If we dwell in the darkness, we contribute to the imbalance, not only in our own personal lives but also in the world as a whole.

For some of us, deciding not to stay fixated on the darkness can be hard. This is a perfect time to ask for support from a therapist, a psychiatrist, an energy healer, family, friends, or from the Spirit world. If you struggle with mental health issues, you need to ask for help. You can ask for help as you feel into and navigate your darkness and for help in not getting stuck in despair.

You may find that your new understanding of darkness naturally helps you. If you remove any shame you have about your struggles, and instead begin to see them as necessary in order for you to shine as a Lightworker, you loosen the grip the darkness has on you. As you begin to welcome and integrate your own shadow, you will find that it doesn't overpower you. Your power and influence as a Lightworker grow stronger as your darkness is embraced.

Release the Fear of Darkness

There are hurting people in the world that bring a lot of darkness with them. Humans can be incredibly cruel to each other, and it is hard to make sense of it. Darkness has no power over you as a Lightworker. You don't have to be afraid. Fear will only create imbalance and allow the darkness to grow.

When you encounter darkness outside of yourself, your role as Lightworker has two parts. First, you refuse to label or judge. This step can be difficult if you haven't fully moved through the previous step of allowing pain to move through your body in order to make peace with your own darkness or trauma. It can also become easier when you understand the darkness has its place. A spiritual perspective requests that you bless the darkness because you know that it can aid in your growth and is needed for balance. Your labeling or judging it is a form of resistance, and your resistance will only cause the darkness to grow in power beyond what is needed to maintain balance. Second, know that you came here to shine and nothing can stop you. Your job is to connect to your Light and let love fill your entire being. When you are filled with Light, there is no room for darkness. You have nothing to fear. Instead of focusing on protecting yourself from external sources of darkness or evil, bring your attention to filling yourself with Light and embodying Divine Love.

TRY THIS

From Fear to Love Meditation

Below is a meditation you can practice that will fill you with Light and bring you back to a place of love. Fear dissolves when we call in and embody love. This meditation can be used to maintain the balance between Light and Dark.

Sit in a comfortable seated position. Say to the fear, "Fear, I see you, I feel you, and you are not allowed to control me." Take a big inhalation and exhale through your nose and relax through your entire body. Come back to your fear again and notice where you feel it in your body. Notice it and feel it. You can say to your fear that you see it and feel it, and watch as it dissolves. Come back to your breath. As you inhale, imagine a pink/yellow Light is activated around your heart center. This warm yellow Light spreads throughout your whole body and you begin to feel Light. A slight smile comes to your mouth. As you inhale again you see the Light expanding out about a foot past your body to create a large protective bubble of pink/yellow Light all around you. You are safe. You are connecting with the energy of love. You see the evil, you see the darkness, and you remain safe as an agent of Light in your sphere of love.

Activation Code

Encoded in these words is the wisdom and power of all the spiritual teachers and healers throughout the ages. The darkness no longer has any power over you. As a Lightworker for these modern times, you are being released from the grip of fear. As you move forward from reading this mantra you will be granted new eyes to see the darkness.

Every time you journey into the darkness, you will come out with beautiful gifts that will enable you to shine brighter than before. You are safe from evil and protected from being fixated on darkness. You are here to restore the balance; the darkness will aid you and never harm you as you shine bright. Your safety is guaranteed.

Affirmations

- I am not afraid of the darkness because I understand we need both Light and Dark to expand.
- I trust life and let go of fear.

CHAPTER 8

SIMPLIFY YOUR LIFE

"Besides the noble art of getting things done, there is the noble art of leaving things undone. The wisdom of life consists in the elimination of non-essentials."

—LIN YUTANG

In the midst of the 2008 financial crisis, I was working for an investment bank. Everyone around me was stressed, all of our clients were stressed, and my workload increased daily. I was taking on negative energy from my work environment and spent many evenings a week attending work functions and trainings. My life was very full, so full I couldn't hear myself think. I had lost touch with the voice of my own soul. Everyone around me was impressed with the work I was doing and I was making more money that I ever had before. I would come home at night exhausted, longing for a simple life—one where work didn't stress me out and I could relax and tend to my own inner healing. I woke up one day and realized I could just say no. I would need to make adjustments to the amount of money I was spending, but I would be able to take care of myself, which was one of my highest priorities. It didn't make logical sense to quit my job, but that is exactly what I did. The result was a simpler life. I didn't go out to eat as much or shop as frequently, but I had ample quiet time to tune into my intuition and care for my soul. I simplified by saying no to what was no longer serving me.

All that is asked of you is that you be a clear vessel for Source Energy to shine through. One of the easiest ways to become a channel of Light is to simplify. We begin to see that all the things we own and all the things we are doing that we thought were helping us or helping others has only begun to cloud the Light inside of us.

If you are ready to step into your calling as a Lightworker you have to be willing to let go of old ways of being, including the belief that more is better. More stuff doesn't necessarily improve your life; it creates more work as you try to manage the upkeep of all that you own. Working more isn't the only way to build the life you desire. More friends, more parties, and more events don't equate to intimacy or depth of community. We have been sold a lie that more is better, and a crucial part of activating your Light is being willing to get rid of anything that isn't serving your highest good.

This includes letting go of the physical stuff, the emotional baggage, and the endless to-do list. It means trading in a life where we are always going, doing, and accumulating for a life that has space for Spirit to work and creativity to flow. Our stuff and our endless obligations steal our energy for what we, as Lightworkers, desire the most, which is alignment with our true essence and the opportunity to share our gifts. Ask your guides to help you imagine ways that you could simplify your life. Ask Source to bring to mind people or tasks that need to fall away. Many of us have a story we tell ourselves about how busy we are and how much we have to do, but we forget that we say yes to everything that is on our list. We busy our days with events that mean little to our spirit. We say yes to activities because we think we should, but our heart is somewhere else. Every time you say yes to something that doesn't light you up, you literally dim your inner Light and deprive the world of your Light. We simplify by only saying yes to what feels aligned and joyful. When we say no to what doesn't serve us, we create more time and space to listen to our intuition, to meditate, to take care of our bodies, and to have fun. All of these things connect us deeply to our Light and for a Lightworker this is the ultimate fulfillment. The quiet moments are when the Light comes in. Have less, do less, and shine more. It's really that simple.

Do Less, Accomplish More: The New Paradigm

We have been told to work hard. A new way is emerging that must be utilized if we are to accomplish the healing work that this planet so desperately needs. For many of us, hard work brings up images of exhaustion, struggle, and pushing beyond our limits. The mantra of hard work served us for a long time. It had its place and many of us have learned a lot from living in a culture where we have been taught this. But it has stopped serving us. Especially those of us who identify as Lightworkers. The hard work has left us burned out, stressed out, and exhausted. Our bodies are screaming for us to stop, as well. There are many reasons for the amount of autoimmune illness we see, but one of them is simply that our bodies are crying for us to do less, to slow down, and to come back into alignment with Source Energy.

If you are reading this book, you are being asked to bravely adopt this new paradigm. Instead of the focus being on hard work to achieve your goals, the focus shifts to alignment. You will find that when you are in alignment and flow, you will actually accomplish more of what you really want to be doing. When you are in alignment with your highest Self, when you have surrendered to a power that is beyond your understanding, you are living in flow.

You trade in hard work for connection to your Light. Yes, there will be work, but it will not drain you, it will Light you up and energize you. If you are exhausted and burned out, you're operating from an old way of being and life is asking you to come back home to yourself and live from a place of deep surrender to the process. Step into the flow, ask for help, and feel the support of the universe.

See the journal prompt below and start saying no to anything you are doing simply because you think you are supposed to or because you feel guilty if you don't. Life will get simpler and smaller, but you'll have more time for the things that really matter. Your life will begin to fill up with people and activities that support you and energize you. You may feel at a loss because it doesn't always feel safe to do less. Sometimes it feels like if you're not always moving, you may die or cease to exist. That is exactly what this process is about. An old version of you does die and a new one is reborn. Dare to do less and trust that you are being guided.

Our path as Lightworkers can be intense, and the journey will take us to places we never dreamed of going. I assure you that traveling light with the people, things, and tasks that bring you joy will serve you and the world you were meant to help heal.

If you are having trouble with organizing your space, or setting boundaries with other people, or learning to say no to activities, this is a perfect time to ask your guides for help. Seek out coaches or healers that can help you learn about boundaries and those who can help you clear out space physically and emotionally. Remember, you don't have to do it all alone. If you need help, ask for it, and then look for the signs and the people who show up in your life when you least expect it to help you simplify. This doesn't have to be a long, drawn out process either. If you are ready to simplify and clear space for Source to flow through you, then this is your time. Get ready for help and get ready for the clearing. Prepare for your Light to shine brighter and the world around you to benefit from the space and clarity you have created.

TRY THIS

Simplify Your Life Journaling Prompts

A great way to simplify is to use your journal to gain clarity. Make a list of everything you do, including cooking, carpools, groups you're involved in, activities, meetings, work tasks, cleaning, yard work, etc. As you look at the list, make note of anything that feels like too much or anything that you think you may need to let go. Use the following journal prompts to gain clarity around where you need to simplify.

- Does it bring me joy and does it serve my highest self?
- Am I holding on to this thing, task, or person because of what other people would think if I let it go?
- How does it feel in my body when I think about it? Does it bring a sense of Lightness to my body, or constriction?
- Am I unwilling to let go of something because I have an underlying belief that without it I wouldn't be OK?
- Am I keeping my life full and busy to avoid underlying pain that I need to address?
- Do I need to learn to set better boundaries?
- Am I willing to say no to opportunities and activities, even if they seem incredible but they aren't feeling aligned?
- Is my sense of worth based on how busy I am, who I know, or what I do?
- Am I willing to let go and live simply so that my Light can shine?

n Code

Encoded in these words is the wisdom and power of all the spiritual teachers and healers throughout the ages. Now is the time for the great clearing and cleansing to begin. Know that whatever no longer serves you will no longer have a place in your life. People, places, and things will begin to fall away. Though you may feel grief, you will be given an unshakable knowledge that you are being guided and that you are on the right path. Source wants you to know that there are many things that no longer serve you and that they are falling away. A new, clearer you is emerging and the Light is filling up your entire being. You feel lighter and free. The details will be taken care of. Thank you for opening yourself up to simplifying. Your Light is shining bright. There is nothing you need to do but clear space for Light and love to move through your being. Shine on, beautiful being of Light. You are clear, free, and full of Light.

Affirmation

- I am ready to let go of whatever isn't serving my ability to activate my Light.
- I trust that by doing less I will activate my Light.

CHAPTER 9

MIND YOUR THOUGHTS

"A person is what he or she thinks about all day long."
—RALPH WALDO EMERSON

I struggled with binging and purging throughout high school and college. I had read books, joined groups, and been in and out of therapy trying to heal from my eating disorder. All of these things helped, and I do think they are an important part of the process. Eating disorders often develop as a way to control an abusive or traumatic experience. Any sort of addiction serves us in the beginning, as it seems like a way to stay safe and self-medicate.

Therapy is important because it can help you understand the underlying trauma that is the root cause of your disordered eating or addiction. I had done all of the things that I was supposed to do to heal, but I knew there was a missing piece. Looking back, I'm not sure what prompted me to do this, but I realized the way to heal was to look at my thoughts. My mind was a prison and I hated thinking. So one day I made a list of every single limiting thought and belief that I had about myself. The list was long. I had an internal dialogue with myself that was full of self-hatred. I called myself fat and ugly daily. I had made up so many stories about my worth being based on what I did and not who I was. The list of my thoughts at the time was on one side of the page and on the other side I wrote a new belief for each that I wanted to adopt. For example, one of my limiting thoughts was "I'll be able to have what I want in life when I look different." I changed this to "I am worthy of everything I need and want now." I took all the new beliefs and cut them up into smaller pieces of paper, stacked them up, and placed them in an envelope in my purse. I didn't have the language or science for it yet, but I was determined to rewire my brain and heal myself. At least five times a day, I would pull out the set of new thoughts I wanted to think and then read them out loud to myself. I read them in the morning, on break at work, on the toilet, before bed, and while cooking. After a few weeks, I had memorized the new thoughts and would repeat them to myself all day long. I was a woman obsessed with feeling better. I had surrendered to my higher power and decided to cocreate a new reality for myself. I began to feel relief almost immediately, and it inspired me to keep going. My new affirmations included thoughts about my inherent worth as a human being and that I was loved and supported always. I told myself that I was safe and beautiful and loved over and over again, day after day. After a few months, I stopped purging, and over the course of the next few years, I stopped bingeing. I'm not going to tell you this process was easy or that it was successful overnight, although I did start experiencing relief almost immediately simply by thinking better thoughts about myself. It was a process. It took a few years to really feel free from my eating disorder, but I would have never gotten to that place without dedicating myself to adopting a new set of beliefs. Today, I think these empowering and beautiful thoughts about myself on a daily basis. I'm also still working on changing thoughts and patterns that are still holding me back.

Every day we are given the choice to cocreate a life that we desire and to join in an ever-changing creative dance with Source Energy. You aren't a victim or a pawn in some political game. Life isn't happening to you, nor is your current situation something you'll be stuck in forever. We can choose to recreate our current reality with some very simple practices.

How Do You Want to Feel?

To join this creative dance, you have to start paying attention to how you feel. When you are feeling good and when you are feeling at peace and in the flow, you know you are in vibrational alignment for what it is that you want to create and attract. This doesn't mean that if you're not feeling good that you push away the intensity of your darkness in order to feel good. It means you pay attention to how you are feeling first. And if there is darkness, you embrace it. You feel it, you move it, and you free it. Then you bring your focus back onto feeling good, on how you want to feel and on coming back into alignment with your highest Self, which is your Light.

This would be a great time to grab your journal and really think about how you want to feel. How do you want to feel when you wake up in the morning and think about starting your day? How do you want to feel when you get to work? How do you want to feel around your partner or around your kids or friends? How do you want to feel after you eat a meal or when you walk in the door at the end of the day? Once you are clear about how you want to feel, it then becomes easier to manifest the reality that you desire. How do you do this? How do you get yourself to feel that way you want to feel? How do you come back to feeling the feelings you want in order to cocreate the life of your dreams? It begins with your thoughts.

You Create What You Think About Most

Your thoughts dictate your feelings. You may not feel like you have control over your feelings, but you can always choose a different thought to influence how you feel. Like attracts like. The vibration of your feelings throughout the day will attract experiences that create similar feelings of the same vibration. You literally create what you are predominately feeling. If you want to see something different show up in your reality, you have to first examine your thoughts, because your thoughts create your feelings and your feelings create your reality. Masters throughout the ages have known that when a man can master his thoughts, he can master his life.

What neuroscience now understands about the brain is that we can literally rewire our brain and form new neural pathways by consistently thinking the thoughts that we want to think. Neurons that fire together wire together, meaning that when you consistently think the thoughts that you want to think, over time they form a new neural pathway in your brain. This results in new beliefs and new habits that will produce a new set of feelings that are more aligned with what you want to create. The National Science Foundation published an article showing that the average person has between 12,000 and 60,000 thoughts per day. Of those, 80% are negative and 95% are exactly the same repetitive thoughts as the day before. The question you want to start asking yourself is, "What are the main thoughts that I'm thinking every day?" You probably have a few thoughts or versions of that same thought that you cycle through over and over again throughout the day. You aren't even aware of the impact that's having on your current reality. One of my limiting thoughts or beliefs that I'm working with right now is "I don't have enough time." I have become aware that many of the thoughts that I am thinking throughout the day are versions of this thought: "Will there be enough time?" "How will I get all of this done?" "I need to hurry up." These thoughts create a feeling of unease, stress, and anxiety, and I find that I then attract more experiences of stress and anxiety. I have been working with changing my belief and rewiring my brain to think, "I have enough time, and I can relax."

You can't have a discussion about thoughts and feelings if you don't also talk about beliefs. Our beliefs are partially influenced by our thoughts and feelings. If you think a thought enough times, it becomes a belief. We build our entire lifestyle and existence based on the beliefs we have about the way things are. When you start to mind your thoughts, you are asked to question what you think, and as a result you will start altering not just your feelings but also the belief system that your life has been built upon. When this happens, some pretty big shifts can begin to take place. These shifts can break you open and lift you up and activate in you a transformative Light that is so bright that people around you begin to heal. It starts with a few simple questions: "Why does it have to be true?" and "How would my life change if I thought a different thought?"

Once you realize that you create what you think about the most, you can start examining your thoughts with a sense of gentle curiosity. You can question whether what you are thinking is true. Does it have to be true? How would you feel if you thought something different? How would your life change if you were able to adopt a whole new set of beliefs and thoughts that affected your feelings and, as a result, your life?

Master Your Mindset to Activate Your Light

Your thoughts and feelings affect your energy field and the energy field of everyone you come into contact with. Negative thoughts and feelings dim your Light. Your internal Light is held captive by your limiting beliefs and thoughts. When you step into your calling and become serious about shining your Light, your mindset work becomes an important part of the process. You are incredibly powerful, and Source Energy flows through you and is a part of you. You have the power inside you to cocreate the wealth, abundance, relationships, and lifestyle that you desire. With this power comes great responsibility. Once you begin to understand the power of your thoughts and feelings and how they have the ability to heal or harm those who cross your path, you have no choice but to pay attention to your thoughts and take responsibility for the thoughts you are thinking.

You don't have to do this alone. If you are ready for a mindset makeover, it is vital that you don't get stuck in the trap of spending all your energy *trying* to think good thoughts. You will stress yourself out if you rely only on willpower to change your thoughts. When you have hit the wall of confusion and exhaustion enough times, you will have no trouble surrendering to the activation process. If you are ready to change your thoughts, you have to put in the work, which I will cover in the next section of this chapter. But you also have to be willing to surrender to the flow of life and ask for help. In your daily practice you can ask Spirit and all the guides that are with you to help you remember. You can meditate and ask for an inner Light to be activated that will help you gravitate toward thoughts that serve you. Change your thoughts and activate your brilliant, powerful Light.

TRY THIS

Thought Inventory

Pull out your journal and make a list of the thoughts you know you think consistently throughout the day. You may not even be aware of what it is that you are thinking. Initially I suggest setting a reminder on your phone every few hours to check in with what you're thinking. Are your thoughts based in fear? Are they negative? Are they true? Once you have collected the thoughts you want to change, make your list. As you read through this list, realize that these thoughts are helping to create your current reality. Now make another list of the thoughts that you want to be thinking. For example, if one of your predominant thoughts is "I'm always tired," you can change this thought to "I am taking care of my body and treating it in a way that will energize me." If you are always worried about money, you can change your thought from "Money is stressful" to "I'm learning how to create abundance and ease with my finances." If you are having trouble thinking of positive beliefs and thoughts to program your mind, I have included a few here for few different areas of life.

Money

- I look for all the ways abundance is already showing up in my life.
- I am opening up the channel for abundance to pour in.
- I love and respect money and I am responsible with the resources I have.
- I love money and money loves me.

Relationships

- I invite in and nurture loving and healthy relationships.
- I deserve to be respected and I set clear boundaries.
- I'm so thankful for the amazing people that are showing up in my life.
- I learn and grow from my relationships.

Self

- I am worthy of love.
- I love and accept both my strengths and weaknesses.
- I know my life has meaning and purpose and I'm excited to be on this journey.
- I am a Lightworker and here to let my Light shine.

Health

- I claim health and healing for my physical body.
- I make taking care of my body a priority because I know my health affects all other areas of my life.
- My body is beautiful and strong.

Career

- I am always being guided and trust I'm exactly where I need to be.
- I'm thankful for my current job and the income it brings me.
- I am excited to live my purpose and be of service, and trust that the next right step will be revealed.

You can come up with many more of your own uplifting thoughts; this list will get you started. After you have the new list made, review it daily as many times as you can. With technology, it is easy to weave this work seamlessly into your day. You can add affirmations as notifications in your phone or download apps with positive reminders.

App Suggestions

Here are some apps I have used and love:

- **Calm**: Positive quotes and affirmations sent to your phone every hour
- **Hourly Chime**: Program in your own hourly reminders
- **#Mindful**: Daily mindfulness reminders
- **I am – Daily Affirmations**: Self-care positive reminders
- **Motivation Quotes**: Daily quotes and positive reminders of the day

You can jot these new positive thoughts down on sticky notes and place them around your house and workplace so that you will see them often. You will begin to notice that as you change your thoughts, the way you feel about yourself and your life will begin to change. As your feelings change to a higher vibration, you will see that you begin attracting more of the experiences and feelings that you want into your life. As you step into your power as a thinker of your thoughts and you begin to mindfully choose what it is that you want to be thinking and feeling, you activate inside yourself an internal fire that will light up every situation you find yourself in. Master your mindset, Lightworker, and let your Light shine.

Activation Code

Encoded in these words is the wisdom and power of all the spiritual teachers and healers throughout the ages. Right now, a desire is being activated in you that compels you to shift your thinking to higher-vibration thoughts. This shift will occur with strength and ease. You will notice that the new thoughts you want to think will work their way effortlessly into your mind. Right now, your feelings are beginning to shift and a new energy is being activated in the core of your being. You are stepping bravely into your role as creator of your reality. Old thoughts are falling away as you usher in a new way of being in the world. A new thought process is being activated in you; your Light is growing brighter.

Affirmations

- I am in control of how I feel.
- I choose thoughts that help me to create the reality I desire.

CHAPTER 10

HONOR YOUR TEMPLE

"The only person who can pull me down is myself, and I'm not going to let myself pull me down anymore."

—C. JoyBell C.

"Accept yourself. Love yourself as you are. Your finest work, your best movements, your joy, peace, and healing come when you love yourself. You give a great gift to the world when you do that. You give others permission to do the same: to love themselves. Revel in self-love. Roll in it. Bask in it as you would sunshine."

—Melodie Beattie

When I was pregnant with my son, my weight climbed up to 200 pounds. I had never weighed so much in my life and laughed in shock when I stared at the numbers on the scale. The incredible thing about being this weight was that I had never felt more beautiful or sexy in my entire life. I scheduled a professional photo shoot at the end of my pregnancy, posing naked in the full glory of my 200 pounds, feeling like the most amazing goddess. I looked amazing, too. People would stop me on the street daily telling me what a beautiful woman I was. Most importantly, I felt amazing because I was taking better care of myself than I ever had in my life. Something about knowing that my body was responsible for the health of another human being changed everything for me. I worked out daily and cooked healthy meals; I gave up coffee and alcohol. I was in awe of what my body was doing. As a woman who had struggled with disordered eating and low self-esteem around her body, my pregnancy was healing me in a way I didn't expect. I realized that the way I had been honoring my body during my pregnancy fostered a deep connection to my spirit and activated an inner Light inside me that everyone noticed. I had the experience of realizing the number on the scale didn't matter. The way I was honoring my body activated my inner Light and that was what mattered most. By taking care of myself, I felt at peace in my own skin and connected to my soul.

As a Lightworker you must prioritize taking care of your body. Many Lightworkers are sensitive and empathic and must pay extra attention to the food they eat, the type of people they surround themselves with, and the amount of stress and noise and violence they encounter. If you are feeling stuck and exhausted, one of the first things to pay attention to is the health of your physical body. Your own inner healing will happen if your body is cared for and you put the needs and desires of your body first.

The Seat of Your Soul

Your body is the key to activating your Light. It's not something to be controlled or punished. Your body is the gateway to your spiritual awakening. Your body holds the information for your healing. Contrary to popular belief, there are no good or bad bodies, there is just your body. Your body is exactly what is needed to house your particular soul. The sooner you begin to see your physical self as the ticket to your freedom, the sooner you will activate massive change in the way you care for your body. Your body shows you where you are blocked and where you still have healing to do. Your body is home to your soul and wants to be treated as a temple for you to live in.

For too long we have seen the body and soul as separate, yet the opposite is true. They are intimately connected and the health of one is reflected in the other. When you fail to take care of your physical body, you send a message to your soul that its needs and desires aren't important. If the body houses the soul and we know that the soul is the most important part of us, then it makes sense that we create a home for the soul on this Earth plane that is beautiful and healthy. Every time you honor your body with the way that you move, eat, or dress, you send a message to your soul that you are tending to its earthly home. This message of care to your body causes your soul to expand and your Light to grow stronger.

Combat Cultural Conformity

It is true that we need to care for ourselves, and it is also important to note that a war is being raged against our bodies, against these beautiful homes for our souls. The war is subtle in some ways and overt in others. It is a campaign of advertising and marketing lies that tell you if you're taking care of your body it will look one particular way, which in our Western culture is young, thin, and often white. We are misled to believe that taking care of our bodies means controlling them with a set of food rules or practices that only result in locking up the soul in a prison of shame and rigidity. We are taught that taking care of ourselves means we trade in pleasure and sensuality for structure and conformity. The very vessels that are the gateway to our greatest opening are held hostage by thousands of companies that have convinced you that you need to buy certain products or look a certain way in order to be correctly practicing self-care. We have been taught that if we make our bodies smaller, it will equal success, freedom, and love. The result of the obsession to become smaller has resulted in squelching the soul and dimming the Light of millions. The time has come to break this pattern of listening to external sources to tell you how to take care of your body.

You are being called back to the wisdom of your own body. You are being asked to develop an intimate relationship with your own needs, to honor your desires, and to embrace pleasure. You are being asked to take back your body from businesses that would use your insecurity to sell you things you don't need. You are being asked to take back your body from a system that wants you to stay sick so that it can profit off your constant state of disease. You are being asked to stop looking at your body as a tool to win status or romance or acceptance. Lightworker, you need to start seeing your body as its own wise entity and the temple for your soul, whose blinding Light will no longer be diminished by a body that is out of touch with itself. It's time to listen to your body and let it tell you what kind of temple your soul wants to live in. This will look different for everyone, but the common thread will be actions that come from a place of deep love and honor for the beautiful temple you call your body.

How Do You Want Your Body to Feel?

How do you listen to your body? You start where you are. You don't have to get to a certain weight or state of health before you can begin to view your body as a beautiful temple. Your body is beautiful now simply because it exists. You listen to your body by paying attention to how it feels. Your journal is your best companion for this. You can make notes about what feels best and slowly create your own personalized self-care plan. You start with identifying your core, desired feelings. You make this list with the help of your soul. Make a list of how you want to feel; maybe it's free, open, healthy, peaceful, strong, light, clear, or energized. With your list of core, desired feelings in place you start testing out what you eat and drink, what you wear, and how you work out or don't work out. You eliminate what doesn't make you feel in line with your core, desired feelings. This process won't happen overnight. So if you're just starting to pay attention to your body, I recommend seeking outside help and support. The process can be simple. Before you do anything that will affect your body, you ask, "How will this make me feel?" When we feel good, we are automatically connected to Source Energy. When we feel good, our souls wake up and start to shine throughout our bodies. Ask yourself, "Am I doing this because I think I should or because my body desires it to achieve my core, desired feelings?"

We abuse our bodies in many ways, often unconsciously. We refuse our bodies sleep for the sake of accomplishment; we deny them food for the erroneous ideal that smaller is better. We tax our livers with substances that impair our ability to think clearly and function optimally. Your body can handle a lot of abuse and still keep functioning, but it is always at the expense of our soul. Normalized abuse of our bodies keeps us from coming home to our true essence and dims the Light that is waiting to burst out onto the world. If you feel stuck, your body will show you habits you need to let go of in order to shine.

Your body holds the keys to unlocking your own healing and freedom. Your body will react to the food and drink that you put into it, and the kind of care that you give it, and help direct you to a place where you can be functioning at an optimal state. Even with the suffering that can be caused from chronic illness, there is a gentle message coming through to try things a different way. Your body is a barometer that will guide you to a place where you can feel good. A healthy body can be a tool to enjoy as much as possible during our short time here on earth. Your soul wants you to live in joy and pleasure and your body can be used to help you achieve that.

You can begin to view your body as the bringer of Light. The Light that is your true essence is carried around throughout the world via your physical body. If you want the world around you to heal through your Light, you have to keep your vessel in good condition. Every time we make a choice to do something that harms or taxes our physical bodies, we dim our Light and we harm ourselves. As we move through the layers of healing associated with our journey as a Lightworker, we will naturally begin to love ourselves more. As we love ourselves more, it becomes harder and harder to treat our bodies with disrespect, because we see the bigger picture and we understand the Light is our true state of being, and that sharing our Light is our purpose.

The way you prioritize your own self-care determines the strength of your Light. I have seen many Lightworkers whose Light is dimmed because they have put everyone else's needs before their own. They may have thought they were serving, but they were really robbing people of their Light because they didn't take care of themselves.

TRY THIS

Self-Healing Practice for Your Body

This practice is an excellent way for you to connect to your body in a loving and healing way. It will give you a way to directly honor your body and help you with intuitive eating and self-care.

1. Sit or lie in a comfortable position. Take a few deep, grounding breaths and connect to your Light. You can imagine a steady stream of white Light is pouring into the top of your head and filling your body with Light.

2. Begin to rub your hands together until they feel warm and then press them together and rest them at your heart for a few moments, calling in a deep connection to loving energy.

3. Start by placing your hands in front of your face for a minute or so and feel the love and comfort of your own hands. You can then move your hands down your body in a way that feels natural to you. Rest for a few moments on each body part that your hands feel led to. Feel the safety, comfort, and love of your own hands.

4. Repeat this practice whenever you are feeling disconnected from your body or you feel like you are being too hard on yourself.

Activation Code

Encoded in these words is the wisdom and power of all the spiritual teachers and healers throughout the ages. A deep tenderness and love is being born in you for your body. Your eyes are being opened to a new way of seeing, your energy is rising, your vibration is rising, and you can no longer treat your body in any way other than with deep nourishment and respect. Already your body is responding to the attention you are giving it and will start letting you know very clearly what does and doesn't work for you. Your temple is beautiful and was given to you perfectly, exactly as it is and exactly the shape and size it needs to be for your Light to shine. You have no option but to shower your temple with love.

Affirmations

- My body is the home for my soul and I love working to create a beautiful place for my soul to live.
- I am making healthy choices that show respect to my body.

CHAPTER 11

DANCE TO HEAL

"If you just set people in motion, they'll heal themselves."
—**Gabrielle Roth**

"Rocking, undulating, swaying,
Carried by rhythm,
Cherish the streaming energy
Flooding your body,
As a current of the Divine,
Oh Radiant One,
Ride the waves of ecstatic motion
Into a sublime fusion
Of passion and peace."

—**The Radiance Sutras**

In my mid-twenties, I was dating a man who was part of a vibrant Sufi community. The first gathering he brought me to was Sufi dancing. Sufi whirling is a type of physical meditation and is a customary practice in their worship as a way to forget ego and connect with the Divine. I had spent years dancing in clubs, never sober. I had never danced outside in broad daylight before. I felt naked dancing without the familiar crutches of alcohol and dimly lit club dancefloors. I didn't know how to move. My body felt uneasy and I ended up sitting off to the side playing with kids. But I was curious. I felt heavy, and it seemed like too much was holding me back from getting up and dancing freely. Something about watching everyone else that day made me feel hopeful, like something was waiting to open up inside of me. I thought that if only I felt freer or lighter, then I could move. What I didn't understand at the time was that dance was the very thing that would free me. The dancing seed had been planted. Sufi dancing is very different from the type of free-form dance I practice now, but the intention is the same: to get out of your head and into your body and to connect with something larger than yourself.

I started dancing a few years later when I was introduced by a friend to 5Rhythms, a healing, meditative form of dance. I was fortunate enough to have some skilled instructors in my early years of dance that helped me get into my body and move in a way that healed me. Years later I had one of my most powerful, healing dances. It was a personal practice in which I set no particular intention for dance, though I did have a strong intuition that I needed to move. The dance became about clearing trauma and negative energy from my root chakra, my pelvic floor. I had done a lot of work at this point around the men I had slept with that didn't serve my highest good. I had worked with clearing out shame and guilt around my sexuality, but there was still more trauma holding me back. Previous to this dance I had been working with a meditation where I was imagining my entire body filled with Light. It was easy for all other parts of my body, but when it came to my reproductive organs all I could see was gray and black. The Light in my meditation would not penetrate my reproductive organs or root chakra. I had been asking for help from my guides and doing everything I knew to clear the energy. This particular practice I'm talking about changed everything for me.

As I began to dance, my body was asking me to shake my hips and thrust my pelvis back and forth. I felt just like one of those animals who was injured and shaking. I remember making sounds and being exhausted, but I just kept moving. I put the song I was listening to on repeat and followed my body's lead. I'm not sure how long I moved, but eventually I fell to the floor in exhaustion. I knew that I had just done some serious energy and healing work. I felt clearer and lighter than I had in years. I immediately went into the Light meditation I had been working with for the past few months and imagined the Light filling up every inch of my body. And that day, for the first time ever, I saw my root chakra, my reproductive organs and pelvic floor, completely filled with and surrounded by white Light. Tears streamed down my face. My body had helped me clear out the last remnants of past lovers and sexual abuse. I marveled at my body's ability to heal and clear and renew. Dance, dear Lightworker, to Activate your Light.

Dance to Release Trauma

We now know trauma is not only stored as a memory in our minds but also as a memory in our physical bodies. As a result, somatic therapy practices like brain spotting, EMDR, and somatic experiencing have been gaining popularity in therapist's offices and addiction treatment centers. The word "somatic" is an adjective that means relating to the body. Research and science have backed up somatic-based healing practices as an effective way to deal with trauma. We have all experienced trauma of some sort. Professionals talk about two kinds of trauma: "big T" and "little t" trauma. "Big T" traumas are life-altering events such as war, sexual abuse, serious injury, or life-threatening experiences. "Little t" traumas include non-life-threatening injuries such as emotional abuse, a pet dying, or divorce. "Big T" trauma is more likely to result in PTSD, but "little t" trauma can also cause a great amount of emotional distress and can result in mental health issues. It is important to be aware of trauma—to name it and stop pushing it aside. If trauma is ignored, it will dim the full brilliance of our Light. Part of our calling as Lightworkers is to heal our own wounds.

If you are suffering mentally and emotionally, asking for help from a mental help professional can be a huge step in your journey of activating your Light. I personally have spent time in therapy and am very thankful for the opportunity and the way it influenced my healing path. I am a survivor of sexual, physical, and emotional abuse. Today I see all of this as a blessing and a gift. My pain forced me into the darkness; the suffering broke me open so that I would know the strength of my own being and the power of my own Light. For me personally, and for many of my clients, somatic therapy (particularly dance) has been one of the most effective ways I have found to move trauma and heal the physical and emotional body.

Humans have been dancing throughout all of recorded human history. Many modern-day cultures have robbed dance of its communal and healing aspects by making it something that is only done in dance clubs under the influence of substances. For millennia, our ancestors danced. They danced when there was something to celebrate, like a wedding or a birth, and they danced when there was something to mourn, like death or war. Our bodies naturally want to move as a way to understand what is happening to us and to process what has already happened. If you watch animals in the wild after they are attacked or injured, you will notice they begin to shake. They shake until the pain and terror is moved through their physical body and then they go on. Humans often do the exact opposite when something traumatic happens. We freeze and, as we freeze, we lock the trauma into our bodies until we hopefully decide to move it out.

Dance is an excellent way to move trauma through our bodies. If you don't move this trauma through your physical system, it will often manifest as addiction, chronic illness, or pain in your body. Dance should be a part of every healing journey. This doesn't mean a choreographed dance step or trying to perform for anyone; this is movement from your soul. This is movement that activates who you are at your core. This is free-form dance, where you follow your inner guidance system to find the steps. You may not even know that you have pain or trauma or anger that you are storing until you start to move. The music picks you up and carries you, and you start to pay less attention to the people around you and more attention to the sensations that are happening in your own body. You lose yourself in the music and movement, and at that moment, an emotion or feeling will rise up in your body. It may be an ache or a tight spot, nausea, or urge to scream. You follow the feeling and move in the way that it wants to move. When moving trauma, you may speed up and shake, yell, or move in short chaotic movements. You simply keep following the feeling and moving how it wants you to move until the feeling is gone and you have left your pain and grief and anger on the dance floor, and then a new feeling arises that you follow.

It is easy to fall into the trap of thinking you have to figure out and analyze everything that has happened to you. Yet this isn't always necessary. Often you can just pay attention to your body and dance how it asks you to. The movement, your voice, and your sweat free you from the very prison you thought you had to think your way out of. You can dance your way free. Your body is your guide. You can trust the way it wants to move even if it feels new or awkward. You keep following your body's directions and move what is holding you back.

If you are new to using dance to release trauma, I strongly suggest you find a trained guide. There are many different groups facilitating healing dance throughout the world. Two organizations that are in many major cities are Gabrielle Roth's 5Rhythms Dance and Qoya. Both of these are great ways to get started on your healing dance journey. If you don't yet feel comfortable in a group setting, I have included steps to create your own home dance practice at the end of this chapter.

Dance to Come Home to Yourself

To dance is to ignite a great love affair with yourself. In order for the dance to have its healing way with you, you must be intimately connected to, and listening to, your own needs. The practice of dance is to tune in to your body, to listen to her cues, her desires, her needs, her longings. The practice is to let yourself feel fully and let those feelings move you. Every time you dance you let your true essence, the reality of your experience, move you. Your dance is a way of honoring your experience. You honor your darkness and your Light and you simply let it all move you. The movement cleanses you and creates a clear channel for Light to move through you. It makes space for new waves of energy to expand you and your experience.

Your dance becomes a moving meditation, a ticket to your own freedom. Once you have danced out everything that is holding you back, everything that isn't truly you, then you are left with the brilliance of yourself. Then your joy moves you on the dance floor. Your movements and steps are filled with peace and ecstasy. Bliss bubbles up from the core of who you are; as you move, you smile, you laugh, you glide, floating across whatever space you find yourself in. You are dancing with your true self and there is no experience that is more fulfilling or exhilarating. From this place of divine union and bliss you enter a space of alignment, creation, and flow. Your Light is activated. This healing, blissful practice of dance is available to all of us when we slow down and tune in to the way our bodies are asking us to move. It is through honoring your body and its desired rhythm that your Light begins to emanate outward toward everyone you meet.

TRY THIS

Create a Home Dance Practice

To cultivate a home practice, you will need a music playlist and some time and space to yourself. You can dance anywhere from 30 to 60 minutes. Go ahead and create your own playlist or search for pre-made playlists. Use your own intuition when picking music. When picking music, choose songs that contain an underlying positive message, ideally from musicians you love. You will want to choose a mixture of flowing and peaceful music and more upbeat songs. I like to start my playlist with music that is slower and will allow me to gently stretch my body and warm up my muscles. Your movements at the beginning may be slower and flowing. You may want to take some grounding breaths and start the process of tuning in and beginning to pay attention to the needs of the body. You can then add songs to your playlist that will encourage you to move more and increase your heart rate; these songs are a good opportunity to move intense emotions through your body. You can add in two or three of these types of songs before coming back to more peaceful flowing tracks to close out your practice. Every dance will be different. You may find yourself full of joy or you may fall to your knees in tears. You let the music pick you up and continue to move you until you feel complete. You can repeat certain songs or add additional songs depending on what your body needs.

After you create a few playlists, you can continue to use them. You may find you like setting intentions for your dance before you move, and you'll find certain playlists will assist your specific intentions. This is your time and your space, and you can trust your body and intuition as you create playlists and dance. You know one thing for sure: You will start the dance feeling one way and end feeling clear. You may not always end in joy, but you will end in authenticity, knowing that you moved your body in the way it needed to move for it to heal and shine. You may want to journal after your dance. If you're dancing solo, you may even have things come up that you want support around from a therapist or friend. You come into alignment and connection with your true essence whenever you decide to follow your body and its desire to move.

Activation Code

Encoded in these words is the wisdom and power of all the spiritual teachers and healers throughout the ages. As you read this, your connection to your body is deepening. Like the whisper of a lover, your body is calling and asking you for something and you listen. You listen with grace and ease and a deep trust in your body's wisdom. Your body has always wanted to move, and today you are granting your body permission to move in whatever way it needs. Nothing can hold you back from shining your Light; you are being given dance to help you heal. You accept it and shine.

Affirmations

- I listen to my body and move the way that it wants to move.
- My body has the power to heal itself.

CHAPTER 12

REPLENISH WITH NATURE

"Man must be made conscious of his origin as a child of Nature. Brought into right relationship with the wilderness, he would see that he was not a separate entity endowed with a divine right to subdue his fellow creatures and destroy the common heritage, but rather an integral part of a harmonious whole."

—John Muir

I have always had a strong connection to trees. When I am with them or sit by them, I intuit information by ways of thoughts and images that the trees want to share. Not long ago, I was on a hike and felt the inexplicable urge to go sit under a particular pine tree. It was massive and way off the trail, and I debated with myself for a while as to whether or not I wanted to make the trek over to it. Eventually, I left the trail and carefully walked over to the tree and sat down at its trunk. I immediately felt a calm come over my entire body and felt extremely alert at the same time. I felt more alive than I had in a long time. It was as if my entire body was lighting up and awakening from the inside out. I sensed that the tree wanted to communicate. Mother Earth wanted a chance to speak. The tree wanted for me to understand something about the nature of reality.

I felt a wave of heaviness sweep over me, a sense of mourning for the trees and our planet. I knew that trees were vital for our survival on this planet, in the way they purify the air and boost our immunity with the natural chemicals they emit. I asked the tree why, why was this happening, why did we continue to treat the earth with such disrespect? Would our planet survive? Would people on it continue to live? Most importantly, I wanted to know what I could do about it. The tree answered so clearly, it was as if the tree were thinking my thoughts and giving me images. The tree said:

The way you help the planet, dear child, is by letting the planet help you. I have so much I want to give you. Energy, inspiration, protection, and healing. My roots are connected to the Source of all Creation. Mother Earth, the source of all life, is getting righteously angry because you are all ignoring that she has the answers to the problems you are facing. Please come sit in nature more and let me give to you. If you open yourself up to my healing and wisdom, you will expand. Your Light will be brilliantly bright and healing will be activated in all people and in the planet. Yes, you have participated in taking from me and you can heal our relationship by letting me give to you. I will never run out of healing and information to give. Mother Earth will actually be healed if millions of people return to the right relationship with her and let her give to them, let her nourish and feed and love them. You see, the more I give, the more powerful I become. The more people come to me and allow me to give, the more I grow and expand and am able to withstand the people that choose to abuse me. Your healing and the healing of our planet and your entire species depends on whether or not people will allow nature to heal them. Don't worry so much about what you have to do; instead concern yourself with allowing me to give to you. I can give you healing, bravery, wisdom, energy, experiences, and information beyond your understanding. You don't have to work so hard to try to save this planet; simply allow me to give to you.

When I felt that the tree was done communicating with me, I was so at peace and relaxed that I couldn't move for at least an hour. What the tree told me was very different than how I had been operating. I had been trying to come up with a solution or be a good enough environmentalist to save the world. The tree was telling me the opposite, saying "come spend more time in nature just sitting," that I needed to allow instead of act. I was shown that nature contains a wisdom that humans did not yet have but that Mother Earth wants to share with anyone who will allow her wisdom to penetrate their being. The tree was telling me the planet will heal itself if we slow down and accept healing. The message was freeing. I wanted the whole world to know. I wanted the whole world to go sit by a tree. If you live in a big city, the trees or little patches of nature that are around your city are particularly in need of humans to give to. You can actually boost the presence of nature in your city and balance the environment by going to wherever you can find trees or grass and opening up to receiving.

Mother Earth Wants to Help

The trees are calling to you; the ocean is whispering your name; the open fields long for you to dance in them. Nature is calling you at all times in a million different ways. The earth has so much she wants to give you: health, healing, food, energy, rest, and information. As a whole, humans are abusing nature, the very entity that patiently waits to help us.

As a healer, as someone who is conscious and awake to the nature of reality, you have been tasked with respecting nature. A person who has activated their Light has a deep respect for nature and is often seen outside: hiking, meditating, walking, playing, dancing, and helping to take care of the planet. Their actions, the things they buy, the food they eat, and the companies they support all reflect a deep love for taking care of the natural world. They realize that nature has much to give them. They realize that nature has played a crucial role in activating their Light and they know that they live in intimate relationship with the natural world. They are dependent on nature in order to shine, and so they protect and love and respect the natural world more than the average person. A person who has activated their Light knows the power and energy that comes from spending time with the trees, oceans, and mountains. An activated Lightworker will receive incredible amounts of energy from nature because they have opened themselves up to relationship with nature and all that it desires to give.

You respect nature by taking care of it and by letting it give to you. Both are important. You can live in a way that is gentle to the environment, but the equally important piece you often miss is letting nature give to you. Nature is asking you to let her help you activate your Light.

Set an Intention to Connect with Nature

If you would like to open yourself up to nature in a new way and allow Mother Earth's healing and wisdom to penetrate you, the first step is to set an intention to connect with nature and receive from her. When you set a new intention, when a new desire is birthed in your soul, one of the most powerful things you can do is to write it down. There is a powerful creative process that is activated when you take pen to paper and declare your intentions to the universe. You may even want to buy a journal separate from your other ones that is dedicated solely to writing down intentions and things that you want to bring into physical reality. List ways and schedule times you may be able to regularly connect and receive from nature. Making time to be in nature is one way you stay connected to your essence, and it is also an excellent way to energize your cells and calm your nervous system.

The second step is to take care of your side of the street by examining how your daily actions affect the environment. Most of this chapter is centered on nature giving to you, but you also need to practice respect for nature. You will find that as you move through this process and begin receiving directly from nature, you will be filled with so much gratitude for the healing and energy Mother Earth brings that your daily actions must change to reflect a kinder way of living in the world. Life in the modern world is centered around disposable plastics and gas-guzzling cars and eating excessive amounts of animal products that take a large toll on the environment. It would be unrealistic for you to stop engaging in any activity that harms the natural world, but you can start making little changes that send a message of respect to Mother Earth. Actions that make a difference include reducing the use of single-use plastics such as cups, shopping bags, or straws; composting and recycling; and riding your bike instead of driving your car. Begin to become mindful of the products you buy, from household products to clothing to kids' toys, because they each have an impact on the natural environment. Be mindful and show respect for this planet that has given so much to us and continues to give.

Third, you have to go spend time in nature, mindful time where you are doing nothing but absorbing the energy and information available there. There is nothing wrong with amazing outdoor activities like skiing, hiking, surfing, or biking. By all means, keep doing those things. Yet you activate a different type of experience when you are in nature being still, meditating and absorbing. There are a million different excuses you can come up with for not finding time to go sit by a tree or lie in the grass. You may even be in a large metropolitan area with limited nature nearby. It doesn't really matter where you go; a park is fine or a tree in your backyard works well. You simply need to make time. Maybe you watch less TV or say "no" more often to free up time. The point is that you have to make time to be in nature. You can start with once a week or once a month, if that feels more doable. When you step into your calling as a healer and Lightworker, you accept that this work is your destiny. It becomes your job and number one priority to keep your channel clear and open so that you can stay connected to your own inner Light.

Finally, when you find time to be in nature, take a few minutes to tune into your intuition and see if you feel called to sit or lie in a particular place or by a certain tree or body of water. Once you are settled, you can simply ask or state your intention to connect with the wisdom of nature and indicate that you are open and ready to allow communication. Maybe you have a question or a problem you are bringing with you. You may just be exhausted and confused and need energy and clarity. Imagine that you are on the table of a massage therapist or energy worker. If you are sensitive to energy, you usually feel the gentle energy flowing through the practitioner's hands to your energetic field. It is the same thing when you are sitting in nature. Nature is doing energy work on you. Your only job is to sit and absorb. Each time you sit you will have a different experience. You may feel subtle healing energy or you may start receiving words, images, or messages like I did in my conversation with the tree. There is no right or wrong way to receive from nature. Your job is to show up and be open. Every time that you mindfully come out into nature to receive, you are taking part in healing yourself and the planet. The more you allow in, the more healing energy, Light, and love expand.

TRY THIS

Refuel Yourself with Nature

The next time you are feeling exhausted or confused, make sitting in nature a priority.

1. Jot down or take note of how you are feeling before you receive from nature. You may feel foggy, tired, overwhelmed, rushed, or angry.

2. Find a tree or water to sit by or lie down in a patch of grass or sand. Aim to simply be in nature for 20 minutes without your phone or any other distractions.

3. Set the intention "I am open to receiving what nature has to give." Focus on the parts of your body that are connected to nature and notice how the energy from nature may enter and circulate through your body. Note any shifts you may feel or information you may receive via your thoughts or body.

4. At the end, notice how you feel different than when you started. Perhaps you are more energized, clear, or present. Thank nature for giving to you freely and sharing its energy with you.

Activation Code

Encoded in these words is the wisdom and power of all the spiritual teachers and healers throughout the ages. You are being called by nature to receive. There is a healing code in nature that is being activated in you now. You find in yourself an inexplicable need to return to nature and in your return you activate the powerful healing process in yourself and for the planet. Mother Earth loves you and desires to start a lifelong love affair with you. You are open to her love and healing. You are healed and whole and an integral part of the expansion and healing of life everywhere.

Affirmations

- I am connected to nature.
- I am open to receiving healing and guidance from the natural world.

PART III

LIVING IN THE
LIGHT

CHAPTER 13

GIVE UP PERFECT

"It is impossible to live without failing at something, unless you live so cautiously that you might as well not have lived at all, in which case you have failed by default."

—J. K. ROWLING

When I started writing this book, I decided to go vegan, give up coffee, and completely cut out any alcohol. I didn't do it because I thought those things made me more spiritual, but intuitively it felt like the right thing to do as I wrote the book. I felt calm and clear as I wrote. My intuition had been right.

As you now know, I have a history of perfectionism, so anytime I decide to completely give up anything, after a while my old addictive patterns of control and perfectionism kick in. I start thinking that I will be OK or worthwhile if I keep doing what I'm doing. I forget that the Light inside me doesn't care if I'm vegan or caffeine-free. After about four months of my vegan, no coffee, no wine journey, I had some fish at a family dinner and I went home feeling bad about myself. This is when I personally knew it was time to let go of the vegan, no-coffee, and no-wine guidelines I had given myself the past few months and live my life with a little more fluidity.

I trust that some people who haven't had the history I have with eating disorders and control would be fine giving up all of the above and not struggle with guilt or compulsion to be perfect. But I do. So I have to be careful with guidelines, rules, and black-or-white thinking around food and spirituality. I have found instead that I must stay closely connected to my Light and my intuition and trust that they will let me know what is right for the period of life that I am in.

So now I'm back to drinking a little coffee, and I'm not vegan, and I'll welcome a glass of wine at a celebration. I find great freedom in the fluid way I choose to live my life, honoring the ebb and flow and being willing to honor my past wounds and still live authentically. I share this story as I close the book to remind you that perfectionism is an easy trap to fall into in life and especially in spiritual communities.

Doing the "Right" Things Will Not Make You More Spiritual

Source Energy doesn't care what you do; it cares about your desire to connect and come home. We live in a world where a form of privileged spirituality has gained popularity. It includes fancy workouts, clothes, meditations, diets, and routines that seem like all the right ingredients for being spiritual. Ironically, these lifestyle choices aren't even accessible from a financial or time perspective for most of the people on this planet. So let go of these images of what "being spiritual" means. The truth is you don't need to do anything or buy anything to activate your Light.

Some of the practices here may support you on your journey. They may be fun to do or you may be able to create beautiful pictures doing them, but the image of looking spiritual is not the goal. You want to feel loved, connected, at peace, and full of joy. This feeling is achieved when you stop caring about doing it perfectly and go back to the basics of an open heart and a simple desire to connect to your Light. All that is required is that you show up and open up. It doesn't matter if you have had the worst day of your life. It doesn't matter if you feel stuck or if you have treated your body or spirit in a way that doesn't serve you. If you show up in life and are willing to connect, Love will find you and flow through you. Some of my most powerful meditations have been on days when I didn't follow any of the guidelines outlined in this book. Show up real instead of perfect, and that is when the magic happens.

What's the Point of this Book?

You may be wondering, "What is the point of this book if it doesn't matter what we do?" Life is full of paradoxes and this is one. It does matter that you aim to live a life that is full of practices that make you feel good so that you can shine your brightest. The guidelines in the Activate Your Life Method are here to help you create a life where you feel most connected to your true essence. If you follow them, you will open a powerful connection to your Light. At the same time, you can go through weeks or months where it seems impossible to follow the suggestions in this book and your Light will still find a way to shine. This is the freedom of the spiritual path that I don't think is talked about enough. You can't mess up. Remove the word "perfect" from your spiritual vocabulary, because there isn't anything you have to do consistently in order to be good enough for you to have the life you came here to live.

Follow the guidelines in this book if they help you feel connected to your true essence. I believe they will help you foster a stronger relationship with the Light. I also believe that the Light will shine through you even on your darkest days. When you think you are doing everything wrong or if you think your life looks dim compared to the flavor of privileged spirituality that is displayed online, remember that these practices are simply an opportunity for deeper connection to your Light.

We forget to tune in when we don't think we are doing it "perfectly," but this is actually the best time to say a prayer or ask for help. As you learn to let go of "perfect," your Light will have a chance to shine. You can't dim your Light on the days you don't think you have it all together. Don't try to start a new routine or eating plan or meditation practice when you are feeling low. Instead, just ask the Light to shine through you and it will, because the Light doesn't care what you do. Your Light just wants to shine through you. All it needs is for your authentic Self to show up and be willing to activate a Light that can bring hope and healing to you and all who cross your path.

TRY THIS

Meditation for Days When You Don't Want to Meditate

1. Lie down on the floor or your bed.

2. Starting with your neck and shoulders, relax each part of your body. Move to your chest, belly, hips, thighs, and down to your feet. Let your body completely relax.

3. Lie down for 5–10 minutes. Nap if you want. If your mind wanders, repeat this simple mantra: *"I invite in more Light."*

4. Bring your hands to your heart and notice how refreshed you feel after a few moments of rest and connection.

Activation Code

Encoded in these words is the wisdom and power of all the spiritual teachers and healers throughout the ages. Your life is right on track. As you read these words, the idea of perfection is dissolving from your vocabulary. You are waking up into more and more acceptance of your beautiful Self. The way is clear; you can never take a wrong turn. Any path you take will lead you home to your Light.

Affirmations

-   I am exactly where I need to be at this time in history.
-   I know that everything is always working out for me.

ABOUT THE AUTHOR
AUBRY HOFFMAN

Aubry Hoffman is an intuitive guide and motivational speaker. She inspires thousands of people all over the world with her weekly podcast, *The Queen of Intuition*, and through her online courses and social media presence. She has a private healing practice that guides her clients back to their true essence and power. Aubry has a degree in broadcasting and is trained as a health coach and life coach and is a registered yoga teacher. She lives in Boulder, Colorado, with her son.

TheQueenOfIntuition.com

ADDITIONAL RESOURCES

Skye Dyer, Singer/Songwriter, Creator of *You Inspire Me* and *Letting Go*, www.skyedyer.com

Rabbi Jessica K. Marshall, Spiritual Counseling and Founder of Sacred Lifecycle Rituals, www.rabbijessicamarshall.com

Andrew Sam Newman, Spirituality for Children, and author of *The Conscious Bedtime Stories Collection*, www.consciousstories.com

Caitlin Gordon, M.S., L.Ac., Functional Medicine and Acupuncture, www.amalunawellness.com

Juniper Jane, Energy Healer at Juniper Moon Healing Arts, www.junipermoonhealingarts.com

Angel Quintana, Founder of *Holistic Fashionista* magazine, supporting 5D Living for the Spiritually Conscious, www.holisticfashionista.com

Christine Walsh, Money Empowerment Coach, www.christinemwalsh.com

Kari Halvorson, Spiritual Counseling, www.karihalvorson.com

Recommended Reading

Sweat Your Prayers: The Five Rhythms of the Soul—Movement as Spiritual Practice by Gabrielle Roth

The Healing Code of Nature: Discovering the New Science of Eco-Psychosomatics by Clemens G. Arvay

The Power of Intention: Learning to Co-create Your World Your Way by Dr. Wayne W. Dyer

Succulent Wild Woman: Dancing with Your Wonderful Self by SARK

Intuitive Eating: A Revolutionary Program that Works by Evelyn Tribole, M.S., R.D. & Elyse Resch, M.S., R.D.

The Radiance Sutras: 112 Gateways to the Yoga of Wonder and Delight by Lorin Roche, Ph.D.

The Law of Attraction: The Basic Teaching of Abraham by Esther and Jerry Hicks

ACKNOWLEDGMENTS

There are many beautiful souls who joined me on the journey as I wrote the guidelines in the book. I want to thank Catherine Gregory for coaching me and turning my dream of writing a book into reality.

For my sister Ruth, you are my best friend and your supportive energy is a part of everything I create. For my mom, who taught me to believe I could do anything.

For Jon, so much of this is possible because of you and your integrity; thank you for believing in me and being one of my biggest fans, and thank you for taking me to the beach so that this book could be birthed through me.

To all the Lightworkers who have influenced me in person or through their books: Ram Dass, Dr. Wayne Dyer, Nova, SARK, Sabrina Ward Harrison, Elena Brower, Neale Donald Walsh, Paulo Cohelo, Sarah Swift, and Gabrielle Roth.

Specifically, I would like to thank Dr. Wayne Dyer for being my very first spiritual teacher. His spirit lives on and was with me while I wrote this book. Thank you for the inspiration for helping me define what an Activated Lightworker looks like in my first chapter.

And finally for all of the people and circumstances who showed me the depths of the darkness so that I would search for and know the strength of my Light.

THANK YOU

Thank you, dear Lightworker, for reading this book. The process of writing was a deeply spiritual one and I believe that I saw many of your faces while sitting in meditation during the months it took me to write this book. I feel connected to you, because I know that at our core we are the same; we come from Source Energy and shine with the same Light. I'm so glad to be walking this journey with you.

You are the Light. I see your Light, and I am excited for the way the world around you will be affected as you step into your calling and activate your Light.

Stay connected with my work on Instagram: @thequeenofintuition.

I would love to hear about your experience with this book and the *Activate Your Light Method,* so please send me a DM and let me know. If you would like to connect with a community of fellow Lightworkers, visit my website and check out my *Activate Your Light* monthly coaching calls.

Find out more at TheQueenOfIntuition.com.

With all the love my heart can hold,

Aubry

The Queen of Intuition

Made in the USA
Columbia, SC
03 November 2019